"Based on a lifetime of attentive reading, keen observation, and thoughtful analyses, Gil Rendle offers us not only a perceptive evaluation of the current situation of churches, but a way forward that emphasizes the *functions* of congregations rather than their *organization*. Arguing that we are in a transition from an 'I' centered culture to a 'WE' centered culture, he urges congregations to be *participants* in their neighborhoods. This book deserves to be carefully read by everyone concerned with the decline in churches in the United States."

—**Gregory E. Sterling**, the Reverend Henry L. Slack Dean and the Lillian Claus professor of New Testament, Yale Divinity School

"Through a piercing and compelling analysis of the current state of things, Gil Rendle summons churches and religious institutions in the United States to the reorientation, resilient revisioning, and robust proactivity necessary to lead and reimagine a hopeful way forward through today's multiple crises. With eloquent urgency, *Countercultural* calls for a rehabilitated grasp of the good of institutions as vehicles through which increasingly isolated persons (and communities) might rediscover the common good, neighborly connection, and life-giving hospitality. There is a dire need, Rendle exclaims, for churches to step up to this moment and live out the simple call of love of God and love of neighbor. Every church and religious leader should read this book, for it is a treasure—filled with astute historical framing, hopeful vision, and practical wisdom."

—**G. Sujin Pak**, dean of the School of Theology, Boston University

"Once again, Gil Rendle, our most able church observer and guide, has written a quite wonderful book for church leaders. *Countercultural* is packed with insights gained from Gil's vast knowledge of organizational and leadership studies combined with his lifetime of life-giving counsel to hundreds of congregations. Gil offers astute analysis of the church's present in order to help the church find its voice in a culture that neither wants nor understands the church. By confronting the ways in which our culture has infected Christ's church with narcissism, individualism, and anti-institutionalism (sorry God substitutes, all) Gil recalls congregations to their God-given purpose and power. *Countercultural* is bound to save many pastors from despair and ignite the ministries of many congregations."

—**Dr. Will Willimon**, Professor of the Practice of Christian Ministry, Duke Divinity School, United Methodist Bishop, retired, author of Leading from the Pulpit: Preaching as Leadership

"In this thoughtful and deeply personal book, Gil Rendle argues that our culture is in a season of 'turning.' Now is the time for faith leaders to come out of the wilderness and re-claim the power and importance of the local congregation. Rendle helps us see what is right in front of us, but not obvious. The church by its very nature is a countercultural institution. He takes us on a journey to show us the simplicity on the other side of complexity, the importance of leaning into the 'We' rather than the 'I,' the discovery of treasure in clay pots and much more. *Countercultural* is the first step on the journey of God doing a new thing."

—**Janice Riggle Huie**, retired Bishop of the United Methodist church, TMF Leadership Formation

"In *Countercultural*, Gil Rendle summons us to subversive acts, first modeled by the Apostle Paul and other early church leaders. These witnesses spoke and behaved God's truth in community, with risky abandon. In doing so, they were captive not to culture or civil religion, but only to the adequacy of Jesus. The result was transformational mission as they lived out Jesus's twin commands to love God and neighbor. Congregations today are called to a similar apostolic passion, depth, and faithfulness. Drawing on the best of organizational and theological praxis, Gil Rendle is a seasoned and articulate guide, eager to show us the way!"

—**Paul Mundey**, minister, consultant writer, former moderator of The Church of the Brethren

"In his book *Countercultural*, Gil Rendle speaks an urgent, clarion call to action for the church to stand to its full height, to be its boldest witness, precisely because the human family, at this moment in our history, needs exactly what a local faith community can offer. Make no mistake, it is not a call to return to the nostalgic glory days of congregations. It is an urgent cry for the church to be courageously countercultural against the strong gravitational pull of a culture bent toward individualism over the common good. In his usual startlingly clear-eyed way, Gil lays out a compelling place for the present and future church. It is hands-down, the most hopeful (and challenging) message I have heard since I entered ministry thirty years ago."

—**Lisa Greenwood**, president and CEO of Wesleyan Impact Partners and Texas Methodist Foundation

"*Countercultural: Subversive Resistance and the Neighborhood Congregation* is as prophetic as it is urgent. With deft historic analysis and exacting insight, Gil Rendle makes a deeply compelling case for the role of the institutional congregation as a 'valuable partner necessary for the present work of humanity.' *Countercultural* is a serious and thoughtful blueprint for healing in our country and our culture which highlights the indispensable role bold and courageous faith communities can and must play."

—**Kerry Alys Robinson**, Executive Partner, Leadership Roundtable

COUNTERCULTURAL

COUNTERCULTURAL

Subversive Resistance and the Neighborhood Congregation

GIL RENDLE

AN ALBAN INSTITUTE BOOK
ROWMAN & LITTLEFIELD
Lanham • Boulder • New York • London

Published by Rowman & Littlefield
An imprint of The Rowman & Littlefield Publishing Group, Inc.
4501 Forbes Boulevard, Suite 200, Lanham, Maryland 20706
www.rowman.com

86-90 Paul Street, London EC2A 4NE

British Library Cataloguing in Publication Information Available

Library of Congress Cataloging-in-Publication Data

ISBN: 978-1-5381-7864-5 (cloth : alk. paper)
ISBN: 978-1-5381-7865-2 (paper : alk. paper)
ISBN: 978-1-5381-7866-9 (ebook)

♾™ The paper used in this publication meets the minimum requirements of American National Standard for Information Sciences—Permanence of Paper for Printed Library Materials, ANSI/ NISO Z39.48-1992.

CONTENTS

Preface

The Framing Narrative

WE MUST ALL CHOOSE HOW WE WILL SEE THE WORLD.

In that choice, we determine for ourselves how we will be in the world.

> *The church is the lens, the template, the framework, the framing narrative through which I see my life and I see the world. The idea and the aspiration of being the body of Jesus Christ and being witnesses to the crucified and risen Messiah is one heaven of a framework through which to see life.*
>
> —BISHOP GREGORY PALMER
> SPEAKING TO THE NORTH TEXAS UNITED METHODIST
> CONFERENCE
> JUNE 6, 2022

An Introduction to an Argument

It is time for the church to speak again.

It is time for the church to speak again because we live in a time of anxiety, and we live in a culture of crisis. In this time of anxiety and crisis, the truth that the church holds is both missing and deeply needed. For reasons to be explored in this book, the church no longer feels that there is a place in the public square for its voice to be heard. Indeed, at the present cultural moment there is considerably less of a public square for any institution to speak and for its voice to be heard. And so, by and large, the church has gone home to talk to itself about itself. But the need is greater than ever for the church to be a neighbor, a good neighbor—a Good Samaritan—and speak clearly about what it sees, what it knows, and what it believes. The church must speak publicly in its own neighborhoods with a conviction that what it says is important.

It is time for the church to speak again.

However, in order for the church to speak again, it will need to understand itself in a different way; it will need to separate out its organizational life from its spiritual purpose, and it will need to address its own sinfulness and lostness. In order for the church to speak again, it will need to stop investing itself in identifying and standing *against* the groups and ideas that it thinks have got it wrong and begin to get clear about what it stands *for* and what it holds that is right. Speaking out about what others do or don't do is not the same as doing one's own work. But, despite all that the church must do to get its own house in order, it is time for the church to speak again about what it knows and what it seeks to be—and without waiting. There is no time to perfect the church, to cleanse it from all sin, or to reorganize it yet again for better performance. It is time for leaders, clergy and lay, to be quietly courageous and bring meaning to this world by honoring God and by loving neighbor. This simple act, well within the capacity of the church, would bring quite a change to a culture that is divided and oppositional. To be quietly courageous and to speak would fulfill the purpose of the institutional church.

In this book, I will argue for the importance of the local institutional congregation (and by extension, the parish, the synagogue, and the mosque) and offer a defense for their role in our communities and culture. The fact is that, overall, our institutional congregations have been organizationally weakened in past decades, have lost their voice in American culture, and, subsequently, have learned to behave as weak and voiceless. Nonetheless, they are deeply needed at this moment primarily because their voice and the life-giving values that they hold are missing from public life. It is an absence that cannot be dismissed without concern at a time of political and generational culture wars that have not only divided us but have made us oppositional as well. If a house (a people) divided cannot stand, there is no time to wait.

Consider a description of our current culture in which the church is absent. In her remarkable and important work, Tara Isabella Burton argues that by this second decade of the twenty-first century there are three "civil religions" that are competing for the hearts and minds of the people in the United States.[1] The first is the *social justice culture*. This is an ideological movement that urges that the "Goliaths" of society (governments, corporations, institutions, and powerful individuals) must be battled or our truest selves will be diminished by their tools of racism, sexism, bigotry, injustice, and an unequal economy. In this civil religion, to be truly oneself means to stand against ideas, laws, practices, and people that would make one lesser than he or she can be. This version of social justice is individualistic and considerably different from the efforts of social justice familiar to the church in which (using a paraphrase from Martin Luther King, Jr.) people have sought to bend the long arc of moral justice to favor the least, the last, and the lost. This is the pursuit of social justice on behalf of others. The new civil religion of social justice that Burton identifies does not stand against the Goliaths on behalf of those who cannot stand for themselves. These are individuals standing for themselves with strong convictions to resist any and all who would define them in ways that compromise or constrain their own agency and sense of self.

The second "civil religion" is *techno-utopianism*, often described as the Silicon Valley culture. This version of a civil religion offers a trust both in "technologically assisted human potential for self-transcendence and in the moral promise of what such a transcendence could mean."[2] Techno-utopianism doesn't see the enemy out there in the issues and -isms that reduce us to less than we are, as the social justice movement does. In techno-utopianism the enemy is within us—in our bodies and minds that make mistakes, get ill, grow old, or die. Harnessing everything from diet and exercise to cyborgian-human enhancements to genetic manipulations to life extension, techno-utopianism seeks to complete, or even replace, our bodies and minds to make us into more than we are and to correct what we are not. While the adherents here are smaller in number than those in the social justice movement, this too is a civil religion of the individual. In both cases, the self is diminished by the enemy—seen by the social justice movement as forces from outside the self, and seen by the techno-utopians as forces from within. In both of these civil religions, purpose is fulfilled when the individual, the self, is no longer constrained from the fullness of what he or she might be. These two civil religions have been quickly monetized through corporate and Internet interests.

The third contender for a civil religion, according to Burton, is an *atavism* that is a throwback to a time when biology ruled: a time when atavists believe men were men and women were women; when white people naturally held power over people of color; when gender was binary and homosexuality was an ill-advised aberrant choice; when authority belonged to the most powerful, and those not in power had only the choice to submit or be thrown into chaos. Atavism is a belief system tied to differences defined by DNA and Darwinism in the believer's mind, two sources that they believe cannot be argued against since they are biologically determined. As such, atavism stands clearly against that which its adherents see as the current cultural sins of progressivism, feminism, and multiculturalism and, at times, is willing to combat those cultural sins with violence. In this civil religion, men who drive trucks into celebrating or protesting crowds, or men who take guns into churches, synagogues, or minority communities are not criminals but heroes. This third civil religion is also an ideological movement, one that has multiple faces. It has found a symbiotic, perhaps parasitic, relationship with the church in an expression as Christian Nationalism. It can also be expressed in forms of survivalism and in multiple conspiracy theories. It is creative in its efforts to constrain others through white supremacy, a radical gun culture, curriculum reform, and banned books.

The civil religions of social justice and techno-utopianism are future oriented, believing in what the self can be if constraints and obstacles are removed. The civil religion of atavism is nostalgic and looks back to what adherents believe the true self was before the interference of progressivism. These may seem to be strange civil religions—although evidence of their existence is easily pulled from the stories in our daily news feeds. But looking at the evidence of how these ideas and their tribal communities have formed offers some further explanation to the political gridlock and the unfathomable violence that pervades American communities in an almost random pattern. One can argue about the status, strength, or the organization of these competing ideologies, but not about their presence or influence. I will argue here that while the voices of these civil religions compete openly in the public square, the voice of the institutional church is largely silent. If heard at all, the voice of the church is more commonly captured by political and market-driven initiatives that distort the church's values and message for their own use.

It was only thirty years ago that Loren Mead made his argument that congregations were the organizational seat of an earlier, widely held Judeo-Christian civil religion.[3] Working predominantly with the leaders of mainline Protestant churches, Mead would remind them that there was no State religion in the United States. And then he would describe how their own mainline Protestant churches were the functioning State church in the nation. In that earlier Christian civil religion (which religious sociologist Will Herberg more fully described as "Protestant–Catholic–Jew"[4]), being a member of a congregation or synagogue was synonymous with being a good citizen and vice versa. To be a good citizen at that time was also to hold membership in a congregation or synagogue. It is not difficult to understand how and why congregations did well during that time when they were so aligned with civic values. For congregations it was a time of organizational growth, of a strong national presence with influence, and, as we were to learn, perhaps ultimately a time of hubris. It is a hubris that congregations and denominations are still trying to sort out.

What holds all of these civil religions together, those past and present, is that they are "religious" in the sociological sense defined by Émile Durkheim as providing the essential components of all religious movements: meaning, purpose, community, and ritual.[5] Each of these civil religions, past and present, provide a story with which adherents could understand how the world works as it does and, thereby, make sense of their own experience. They each give their adherents a role to play in the world that they thus can understand; a supportive community of others who see what they see; and a standard of actions, practices, and celebrations that mark them as a believer.

What makes the three current ideologically competing civil religions described by Burton different from the former Judeo-Christian civil religion is that the current civil religions are decoupled from any creeds or claims about God. Each of them, social justice, techno-utopianism, and atavism, make arguments about the individual, the self, as sufficient without claims to powers or purpose beyond the individual. Each offers a story of how the world is and what constrains or blocks the individual from becoming the "true self" that each is meant to be. There is no concern for the common good that holds all people together, for the neutral public space where people can engage each other with mutuality, or for a purpose that goes beyond the present moment and the singular self. It is time for the church to speak again.

It is important to understand that the three current competing civil religions are each anti-institutional as well. This anti-institutional stance may be one of the most critical facts to keep in focus when considering the importance of institutional congregations and our present need for them in our personal and communal lives. The singular focus on the "self" that is held by all three of the civil religions positions them against institutions. For institutions, by definition, form us not only as individuals but as communities as well. Institutions, particularly the institutions of morality, like congregations, give us ways by which we can live with and value others. They do not focus with exclusion on the self. Instead, they speak of the importance of the other, the common good, and at their best, what brings us together rather than what divides us.

Moreover, the institutions of morality give us disciplines to follow—guidelines for loving one's neighbor, practices for caring for those wounded, ill, and set aside to the margins of society. They give us disciplines of generosity to share with those who have less. Such disciplines that direct us to reasons and practices that include others are by their very nature constraints on the self. If one's civil religion of choice, if the way in which one chooses to see and understand the world, is based on an ideology of the self and the quest to be as truly one's own self as possible, such institutional disciplines can only be experienced as a constraint to be avoided—as an enemy of the self.

The reality is that the American culture has been moving in the direction of the individual for some time, a topic to be explored in a later chapter. An expanding economy, the marriage of technology and marketing, and a consumer-based corporate culture have moved us steadily toward a singular attention on ourselves as individuals. Perhaps most influential has been the corporate and social media use of the Internet. Each time civilization has gone through a breakthrough shift in the means of communication—from the printing press to broadcast radio and television to computers to the Internet—we have experienced major resets in human relationships, education, work, and religion.[6] Robert Bellah helped us see as early as 1985 the emergence of newly shaped religious faiths such as "Sheilaism," which was an example of a communication-based reset of religion self-shaped by just one person for her own use. Bellah provided a description of how a woman named Sheila shaped her own personal version of a religious faith that best suited her own comforts and needs.[7] Such an individualized religion was possible because of the ability to draw information and ideas from many multiple sources filtered through that person's own personal therapeutic self-understanding. By the turn of this century, Burton gives evidence of what she calls "bespoke" religions. "Bespoke" is an older English word from the seventeenth century that was once used to describe tailor-made suits and shoes commissioned for a specific individual. Today's bespoke religions are similarly commissioned to follow particular specifications in which individuals can pick and choose which parts and pieces of a mix of traditional world religions, generational preferences, and cultural trends they would like to weave together for their own spiritual use.

It is an oversimplification to dismiss the individualistic spurning of traditional religion and the cut-and-paste bespoke religions of today as the rise of secularism over religion. The human interest in, and need for, religion has not at all diminished in our technological age. What is deeply embedded in and consistent throughout all of what is described here is an unending and uninterrupted search for meaning in life that has been intrinsic to humans throughout time. As early as 3100 BC (that is to say, beginning more years before the birth of Christ than humans have since lived after the birth of Christ) the inhabitants of the Shetland and Orkney Islands in the North Sea, above what today is Great Britain, raised massive stone circles and constructed henges.[8] Still not fully understood, what is clear is that the placement of these stones into circles and henges were in response to, and explanatory of, nature. It was an early effort to understand and explain how humans lived in a world controlled by forces of nature well beyond themselves. They were telling a story of how the world was as it was, what their place was in that world, and how to gather together for support and to ritualize what they knew. The subsequent world religions, the current contesting civil religions in the United States, and the contemporary bespoke individual spiritual expressions still stand in the same lineage of that very same quest for meaning that has never left us, and which we have never left behind. Secularism in the present age has not diminished this quest by the individual in the least. It has simply helped this search to find different forms.

Explanations for how the world is as it is, and our place in it, are still of highest value to humans. In our given moment in history the rate of change overwhelms, making the search for meaning even more critical for a people overwhelmed. Information expands at an exponential rate, making trustworthy facts even harder to find. Power itself has been redefined, shifting control and authority to surprising—and surprisingly small—agents and agencies in ways that now throw national and global stability into chaos.[9] At contest now is what all this change means, who will benefit, what will be most valued, and how we will each live best in a yet unpredictable future. What now can we say about how the world is as it is and what our place in it might be? Our circumstances of living have changed dramatically, but our questions of meaning have not.

Let's get specific for a moment and connect this description of competing civil religions to actual events in our world as it now is. As I was writing this introduction, I was in Texas not far from the town of Uvalde, where a young high school student shot his grandmother and killed nineteen elementary school children and two of their teachers. Since 1998 there have been over 100 mass shootings in the United States in which four or more people have been killed. The next highest count of such mass killings is in France where, again since 1998, there have been eight such shootings. Clearly, a "gun culture" that allows for such a superabundance of multivictim shootings is a United States issue. It is a simple, necessary act of courage to insist that we ask what messages a young, high school boy might have been hearing in US culture that would cause his anger, depression, or despair (or what?) and lead him to take violent action with an assault rifle against people, most of whom he did not know. I have no way of knowing, nor does anyone else.

But perhaps, in his despair, this young boy heard the marketing voices of the self-care industry and realized that he could never be thin enough, handsome enough, athletic enough to gain the appreciation and recognition he wanted, or escape the bullying that he experienced. Or perhaps he had been listening to the voices of the competing civil religions and realized that the Goliaths had stacked the deck against him, making education hard to get but guns easy to acquire, or that he would never have the resources needed to afford the technology that could make his future different, or that he didn't fit into the white, male cohort to whom the world is supposed to belong. Or perhaps family failed him, providing little support, direction, or stories of hope that would encourage him on. Or perhaps he fell down one of the dark holes of the Internet that gave him a picture of a world that he didn't want to live in. Or perhaps . . .

What can reasonably be argued is that a young man such as this was less likely to hear and believe that he was a child of God, equal to all other children in creation, and that life's purpose was that he was to be loved and to love others. This Christian narrative is far from a Pollyanna story glibly offered as substitute to harsher realities. It is a real alternative way of seeing the world and living in the world that is grounded in history, lived by millions, and based on real disciplines of daily behavior. It is a narrative for which there is currently little public space, making it harder for it to be heard by anyone.

Many Christians and congregations will again rise up after the Uvalde shootings to demand that legislators do their jobs and pass gun control laws, to protest a gun lobby out of control, to blame communities and schools for not providing sufficient social services, and to wonder about parents and families that don't provide both the encouragements and restraints that would preclude guns as a means of dealing with an untenable life. But Christians and congregations must also be challenged. The work of legislation, the work of bringing restraint to lobbyists, the work of providing social services is actually not the work of the institutional congregation. That is all work that belongs to others while congregations must be encouraged to do their own work. Blaming others for what is not done to make a livable world may actually be work avoidance by the institutional congregation too timid or too confused to do their own work of making their voice heard in the public square and taking their own actions of care for the welfare of the children closest to them in their own neighborhoods.

In this book, I will argue that the institutional congregation need not be a weak agent easily dismissed or ignored in our current anxious search for present and future meaning. The institutional congregation is a valuable partner necessary for the present work of humanity. However, to be a worthy participant, congregational and denominational leaders will need to step away from their feelings of weakness and timidity. They will need to admit the hubris inherited from recent generations and also face their own role and participation in the sins and injustices of racism and sexism, as well as their less than holy alignments with politics that have made them untrustworthy. And, in order to move forward, they will need to release themselves from their hobbling anxiety over their decreasing memberships, shrinking resources, and generational aging. Quietly courageous leaders will need to identify, reclaim, and once again offer the values and truths on which they were originally founded. The better part of the work that now faces the institutional congregation will be addressed by reclaiming the purpose for which they are again now needed.

Institutional congregations, at their best, already hold an ancient, important, and compelling story of how and why the world is as it is and what place we, as individuals, have in that world. It is a story that, unlike today's competing civil religions, includes the "other," includes the common good, and includes an understanding of a common and universal origin by the singular and shared creative hand of God. As far as explanations of meaning and stories of purpose go, this is not a worldview that we want to move into the future without.

It is time for institutional congregations to understand their purpose and power again—and not confuse these with their organizational status or their cultural acceptance. It is time for the church (and the synagogue and the mosque) to speak again and to point to what the culture is now having difficulty finding.

In Defense of a Countercultural Church

FOR TOO LONG CONGREGATIONS AND THEIR DENOMINATIONS HAVE struggled to fit into this changing culture. The post–World War II era presented itself as an historically high watermark of community and cultural cohesion in which congregations thrived. Certainly not everyone (especially blacks, Hispanics, Asians, and people who identify as LGBTQ+) was folded into the cultural cohesiveness with equality and warm welcome. Those kept to the margins of what was then presented as a new national unity were required to keep their differences and their exclusion muffled and hidden. As we move forward in this present argument, which is heavily anchored in the ways in which cultural values continually shift, the incompleteness of the actual unity of the eras that were driven by racism and sexism must be recognized as a persistent counter theme. We will come back to this discomforting truth a number of times as this argument moves ahead. Nonetheless, the post–World War II era was a time marked by a widely held sense of unity and a shared national identity. It was, as well, a time of a greatly expanding economy. After the destruction of European and Japanese manufacturing during the war, America emerged in a position to provide more than 50 percent of the manufactured goods to the world. Resources were abundant. As Thomas Friedman pointed out, it was a time in which a rising tide bore all ships afloat.[1] It was an "additive" moment. Resources were so abundant, participation was at an all-time high, and almost anything that people could dream of could be added to the list of "priorities" to be dealt with. Indeed, the word "priority" lost its meaning for a time since so many resources and people could be thrown at multiple needs or interests, and nothing needed to be taken off of the list, thereby making both everything and nothing a priority. Whatever people sought to add—new businesses, church buildings and programs, community volunteer organizations, public parks, and expanding urban and residential infrastructure—the answer was "yes." Growth was normative, and many businesses and organizations, including congregations, were carried along with the rising surge. Because this time of national growth was misunderstood as a sustainable norm rather than the aberrant period that it was, the hubris that settled into national, community, and congregational leaders has overshadowed and complicated the reality of the current moment.[2]

However, at that earlier post–World War II time, congregations stood at the heart of American culture, both as an institution and an organization (a distinction to be made later). More than just fitting in, as noted above, Judeo-Christian congregations were at the heart of the civil religion of that day.

Beginning in the mid-1960s, the tide shifted and congregations found themselves in a much-changed cultural context. The American culture was beginning its next cycle of an ongoing oscillating swing in the tension between the cohesive values of community and the non-cohesive values of the individual. This swing of cultural values is critical to understand and will also be explored in a later chapter. The consequence for congregations in this swing was to be left with a sense of confusion (asking why what once worked so well didn't work anymore?) and a diminished voice and feeling of impotence (asking why the congregation's voice didn't carry as much authority anymore?). Within the lifetime and experience of many people of the early Baby Boomer generational cohort (1946–1954), of which there are still many, the congregation went from being the locus of values, family formation, and social gatherings to being a diminished voice in a cacophony of voices, activities, and choices in which few were more important than the others.

None of this suggests that Christianity has lost its force or centrality as a way to live a generous life under the creative hand of God. Nor does it suggest that there aren't some thriving, vital congregations still in mission and ministry in their communities. There continue to be examples and demographics of congregational vitality as some congregations have learned to accommodate the cultural changes around them—often with rather entrepreneurial inventiveness.

Nonetheless, the dominant story for mainline and evangelical congregations, Jewish synagogues, and Roman Catholic parishes has been learning how to live in a harsher, less welcoming environment. In each of these religious systems there are more congregations that are shrinking in size, merging, and closing than there are congregations growing or starting up new. In most of these systems, the diminished flow of resources has deferred building maintenance, curtailed staff and programming, and shortened the anticipated lifetime of the established congregational organizations. There are fewer adults choosing to go into congregational leadership as a profession and fewer congregations able to afford the compensation package of those who do choose to be in full-time ministry. The swing of cultural values that we have been through has produced a byproduct of diminished congregational systems and an attending rise of anxiety among the leaders of those congregational systems.

During this period of changing values from the mid-1960s through the present day, the primary agenda of congregational leaders has been to seek ways to fit in with the cultural changes. I was in seminary in 1969, ordained and serving as pastor in a local church by 1972, and have spent my adult life in congregations as pastor, consultant, teacher, researcher, and participant. In an earlier writing, I reflected on my own path through the worries, anxieties, strategies, and learnings of congregations as they sought to fit into their changing surroundings.[3] I can recount the path of congregations through programs of church growth, redevelopment, revitalization, relocation, strategic planning, vitality; contests over the theologies with the best cultural fit; and internal culture wars over music, liturgies, times and venues for worship, and appropriate clergy garb. It has been a rather extended attempt to learn how to fit into and be more welcoming to a culture that was changing around the congregation.

THE SUBVERSIVE RESISTANCE OF NOT FITTING IN

What I want to argue in this book is that it is time to change the agenda of the congregation. We have, for the most part, learned what we can about fitting in and capturing as much "market share" of adherents for our organizations as we can in an arena of cultural competitors. I want to be careful to state my conviction that what congregational leaders did and learned during this time, beginning in the early 1970s, has been worthy work. It has kept Christianity present in our changing culture, allowing us to be adaptive without being overly syncretistic. It has helped us to keep our focus on our faith and how to share it. Perhaps most important, it has presented questions that should never be sidestepped, such as, "Who are we now?" "What does God call us to make different now?" and, "Who is my neighbor now?" No person or organization can hope to thrive without a willingness to ask—and answer again and again—these most basic questions of identity, purpose, and context.[4] This was work done well by able leaders in a difficult time.

However, it was the work of "fitting in." It was work seeking ways to participate in the culture as an equal, or at least as another voice in the mix. I now will argue that fitting in is neither the only, nor most important, agenda for the congregation. The church needs to choose a different relationship to the culture. Indeed, determining the appropriate relationship between the church and the culture is a perennial task as so clearly expressed by H. Richard Niebuhr in his 1951 classic, *Christ and Culture*.[5] Niebuhr wrote to Americans coming out of World War II who had learned how to stand together against a State leader who had been elevated to semidivine status. He was addressing how citizenship and faith fit together. It is a question as aged as the politically astute conversion of the Roman Emperor Constantine in the fourth century, by which he made all citizens under his rule to be Christian as he was—thereby bringing the church and the culture together as one. It is a question that is ours again. Should the church fit into the culture? Or should it stand out?

I now argue that this is *not* a time to fit in any longer. The institutional church is, by its very nature and purpose, a countercultural institution. I am writing this from a Protestant perspective as a United Methodist clergyperson, and so my language easily finds its place in words like "church" and "congregation." But a religious faith, by definition, is countercultural in positing power and agency outside of any reigning political or economic system. So, what will be explored in this book, by extension, also belongs to parishes, synagogues, and mosques. Faith in all of its institutional and organizational forms is countercultural in its intended focus on God and on the other (the neighbor) and seeking a way for the individual to extend beyond the limits of the self to be in relationship with both God and other. It is countercultural in its disciplines and practices that need not be overly rigid but are, nonetheless, not options to be chosen or dismissed according to the preferences of the individual. It is countercultural in seeing differences as enriching rather than dividing and seeing the common good and shared public space as necessary to both the life of the individual and the life of the planet. At a moment when there are strong competing civil religions all claiming their space in the public domain, it is not time for the institutional church to fit in but to stand out. Our nation—and the people of faith in our nation—now need a voice that is deeply countercultural. As will increasingly be seen as we move ahead, being countercultural is a subversive resistance to the way our culture is currently moving—a life-giving gift that can be borne by courageous congregations.

Yes, of course! How could anyone begin to explore this countercultural nature of institutional congregations without admitting the host of examples of currently established congregations doing this work poorly, or not at all. Congregations, like all human organizations, are subject to mission creep, subject to the temptations of member preferences over missional purpose, and naive to the difference between their political world and their spiritual world that makes them subject to political manipulation.

But there are particular times in which a culture needs institutions like congregations more than they do others. I will argue as we go along that American culture is at a turning. It is a time in which the very values that lay at the foundation of our individual, communal, and national behavior are in contest. This is not a time in which our institutions of morality can allow their voices to be minimized or to withhold the truths they lay claim to. Congregations cannot now be constrained either by their mismatch with the culture or by the anxiety of their leaders. This is not a time to too carefully fit into a culture that is seeking to turn. It is rather a time to stand out as countercultural to where we currently are as an American people so that new hope can be seen.

THE TREASURE WITHIN

In his second letter to the church at Corinth, Paul wrote about his hardships and punishments in a way that now seems metaphorical for the American organizational congregation over these past decades. He wrote, "We are experiencing all kinds of trouble, but we aren't crushed. We are confused, but we aren't depressed. We are harassed, but we aren't abandoned. We are knocked down, but we aren't knocked out" (2 Corinthians 4:8–9). The reason that Paul could encourage his followers to be in trouble but not crushed, confused but not depressed, is clearly stated in the verse that immediately preceded this description:

> *But we have this treasure in clay pots so that the awesome power belongs to God and doesn't come from us.*
> 2 CORINTHIANS 4:7

This is equally metaphorical for the American organizational congregation as well. There is the clay pot—the very earthly organizational, denominational, and personal way in which the congregation goes about its activities. It is this clay pot that leaders have been so anxious about because of the loss of membership and resources. It is this clay pot that has been working so hard to fit into a culture that, quite naturally, has understood it less and less and, thereby, afforded it less and less attention and resources.

But in that clay pot is a treasure. It is a compelling truth, a worldview that goes far beyond the competing civil religions of the day. This treasure held by the congregation is a story of meaning that does not fit into the current contests of the day. It stands apart—sharply countercultural—which is exactly why it is needed again. The treasure of the Kingdom of God is countercultural because it stands apart from the competing kingdoms of this world and their civil religions.

This differentiation between clay pot and treasure helps us to understand why our present congregational organizations can be weakened at the same time that our faith is strongest and most needed. In order to be truly countercultural, our leaders will need to embrace this distinction between pot and treasure—between the organizational life of the congregation and the institutional truth of the congregation. The clay pot of the organization is under great stress and may not live into the future in the same shape, with the same role, as it has in the past. Indeed, in the next chapter we will see that over the brief history of America from its founding this is as it has been all along. The form and the role of the organizational congregation has shifted and morphed, as necessary, to its changing times. Over-preservation of a particular form of a clay pot makes it into a museum piece when it was always meant to have far greater utility. To be of use, the shape and function of the pot must undergo the stress of use that will eventually wear it down and make way for the next iteration of the pot that will be better shaped for its needed function.

The next shape and function of the congregation will come in response to the truth it holds and the purpose it seeks—its treasure all along. The work of discovery to find this next shape and function is already well along, both in the current congregations that have learned to thrive in this culture and in the entrepreneurial experiments that look very uncongregational from the outside. To follow this work of discovery and to live with strength as Christians in the next cultural turning, there is additional learning to be addressed, to which this book seeks to contribute. Leaders will need to be clear about the ways in which the form, structure, and behavior of congregations have historically been fungible and must now be flexible and interchangeable again. Leaders will all need to be clearer about the blind alleys our culture now finds itself in, the stresses created by dominant cultural voices seeking control, and the nature of cultural values under stress in search of new direction. It is now very difficult for leaders of any organization or movement to find the next steps on the ground without a reliable 30,000-foot overview to provide direction. While it may seem somewhat esoteric to speak of cultural values in the ways we will in this book, the reality is that we are speaking of worldviews and principles that guide daily behavior and relational connections. To move ahead, leaders must have a better sense of the reasons beneath the odd, contesting, sometimes violent daily behavior by which we, as an American people, are looking for our better future.

Above all else, for leaders of congregations there must be a firm and clear appreciation for the value and the importance of an institutional congregation in a very anti-institutional time. Being clear about the difference between the *organizational life* and the *institutional value* of a congregation is critical and will be addressed in a later chapter.

However, to offer some initial insight about the importance of the institutional congregation, let us begin by recognizing that there has now been a significant groundswell in conversation about tyranny and fascism since the 2016 presidential election in the United States. Lest we too easily think that this is connected only to our own national politics, consider that the swing toward a populism that has raised fears about tyranny and fascism has, in fact, been global, encompassing both the northern and southern hemispheres, developed and undeveloped nations. Populism, tyranny, and fascism are not ideologies. They do not offer a way to understand the world as it is or help us to find our place in it. They simply seek control for those who hold the most power and resources. And institutions are a part of the antidote. Timothy Snyder, professor of history at Yale University, offers twenty brief and quick lessons from twentieth-century history on how to stand against tyranny. Lesson number two is "Defend institutions."

> It is institutions that help us to preserve decency. They need our help as well. Do not speak of "our institutions" unless you make them yours by acting on their behalf. Institutions do not protect themselves. They fall one after the other unless each is defended from the beginning. So, choose an institution you care about—a court, a newspaper, a law, a labor union—and take its side.[6]

I choose the congregation and will seek to defend it thoughtfully for what it can be, not blindly for what it has been. This book is an invitation for you to do the same. As our culture stumbles ahead through the contesting worldviews and civil religions that want to provide their own answers, the countercultural congregation is both an antidote to what we have become as well as an engine to move us ahead to what we could be. It is time for congregational leaders to reconsider the power and importance of the local congregation. It is time for the church to speak again.

CHAPTER 2

What Now Is a Congregation?
The Hidden Malleability of the Institutional Congregation

FOR CONGREGATIONS TO CLAIM A NEW COUNTERCULTURAL PLACE IN A turning culture, a primary step is understanding that the organizational congregation is malleable—being able to adapt and transform as needed to fulfill its purpose. Congregations appear to be steadfast and stable organizations. However, throughout the history of America, congregations have shifted and morphed in both organizational form and function to accommodate the context in which they existed. Congregations are tradition-based, voluntary associations that feel almost intransigent for leaders who are trying to change them at any given moment. But while slow to change, over time, congregations naturally morph to accommodate the cultural context that influences them from the outside. This is the history of congregations in America, where congregations have shifted their shape and role multiple times since before the founding of the nation. It is a slow process of accommodation and, therefore, not easily seen by the people who are living in the congregation day to day. It can, however, be seen by beginning with our own experience of congregations, then considering the changes visible from an historic perspective. First, consider the way in which congregations naturally adapt in resilient ways to the continuously changing demands of successive generational cohorts.

As a young boy I would sit next to my grandfather, Henry Firestine, in worship at the First Congregational Church in the little town of West

Pittston, Pennsylvania. Henry was a conductor on what was then the Lehigh Valley Railroad—the railroad he began to work for at the age of thirteen when he left school, retiring from there many years later. He was, in my memory, the most fun person in the family, even in church.

Attending worship at First Congregational Church with Henry and my grandmother, Bessie, only happened when we were visiting, but if the visits to First Church were sporadic, what was steady and dependable was my grandfather's church joke. I knew I could depend on getting a nudge in the ribs by my grandfather's elbow at some point during the preacher's sermon when the sermon tilted toward the sinfulness and depravity of humanity. Getting my attention with his nudge, my grandfather would very quietly point at the preacher and then at me, whispering, "He's talking about you." At a young age I was learning that even the most repeated jokes don't necessarily lose their humor, and I'm sure I listened even more intently to the sermon trying to guess when I would get Henry's poke and whisper.

What was as predictable as my grandfather's joke was the Sunday noon conversation over lunch when morning church was debriefed and debated. Who was present and who was absent was noted. Some conversation was given to why particular hymns were chosen and others were not. The controversy over how the preacher had tried to move the baptismal font outside of the chancel rail the previous summer was rehearsed again (and again and again)! The board's proposal to rent the social hall to a non-Christian group was debated with some energy. And the list of people needing prayer and special consideration was reviewed, with necessary details and stories provided.

What I was experiencing was the work of a congregation as a mediating institution for people who lived in stable communities where they shared their faith across generations. The congregation was mediating the hopes, needs, and practices of the faith that was shared between the people in a given community and between generations. As such, it was functioning as described by Dorothy Bass as the "bearer of tradition."[1] She noted that a primary function of a congregation was to simply bear the tradition of the faith from one generation to another. To do this, explained Bass, congregations used two primary tools: argument and accommodation. The people would argue about what they experienced: the choice of hymn, the preacher's attempt to move the baptismal font, the appropriateness of a non-Christian group using their facilities, the inclusion of a particular man's name on the prayer list given the consensus that his own behavior had, in fact, been much of the cause that had ended his marriage anyway. The people would argue during Sunday lunch (and beyond) with points made and positions taken.

Then they would accommodate one another with some level of agreement so that their arguments did not divide them. In the process small changes would begin to mount up—the list of acceptable hymns broadened, the specific and temporal location of liturgical furniture became a little less sacred, the use and purpose of church buildings was stretched a bit beyond a limiting parochialism, and the strict lines and assumptions about moral behavior would be either relaxed or tightened. In the process the modest changes of tolerance and adaptation made the tradition and practice of the faith ready for the next people. The local congregation was mediating change that would allow the faith to be passed on in a more suitable, usable form to the next generation.

Stories such as mine about congregations are still fairly common in the memory of older generations of Americans because congregations once played a central role in the lives of families and communities, where up to three generations commonly sat side by side in worship week after week. Those congregations once monopolized the lives of their members, not just through worship but through recreation, education, child care, family life, vocational decisions, and personal identity. For many, the congregation was a comprehensive institution giving primary shape to how the individual would live his or her life, as well as give shape to how life was to be shared with others in the greater community.

For many older people, this model of a congregation as a central, all-encompassing, mediating institution is the dominant way they continue to think of congregations. It is also, for many, the nostalgic focus that prompts anxious questions of how to return their congregation to that once central location in the lives of people, for clearly, congregations are not the central institutions giving shape and meaning to lives that they once were in many people's memories. Nostalgia runs strong among people who sense that they have lost something of value.

THE LARGER HISTORICAL CONTEXT

While the local congregation could go through slow and modest adaptive change to accommodate the shifting preferences of successive generations, it is also important to see the larger cultural changes that the organizational congregation has negotiated over time. Gibson Winter, professor at the University of Chicago Divinity School from the 1950s to the 1970s, noted the breakdown of this central cultural role of congregations as early as the 1960s when he wrote about the "suburban captivity" of the church.[2] He argued that the congregation was becoming "an organizational church," reacting to the increasing mobility of Americans by seeking loyalty through participation in programs, activities, and governance. Communities were becoming less stable and congregations less central. Three generations of people in the same family no longer lived as neighbors in the same towns and, therefore, did not regularly sit side by side in shared congregational pews. From this perspective, congregations were simply becoming less important to people as an institution of family and community cohesion or as a bearer of tradition. From Winter's view, congregations were being transformed by the new patterns of population movements. In response, they were substituting committees, activities, and events for the sacraments, the teachings, and the formation of lives that were central to the once stable community congregation. No longer a mediating institution reshaping faith to be passed along with continuity within stable families and communities, congregations were learning a new and different role of providing an anchor and a social base for a mobile people within fast-changing communities. This was a cultural shift requiring larger changes in role and organization, compared to the ongoing mediation of generational preferences. What was being lost and what was being gained, as institutional congregations shifted in their roles, was highly debated. What could not be challenged was that the role of the institutional congregation was shifting. Its place and purpose for the individual, the family, the neighborhood community, and for the overall common good was morphing in a way that felt like a loss to some while simultaneously meeting a need of others. What was clear was that the organizational congregation was not the stable, intractable, unchangeable thing that so many thought it was. In fact, it had never been.

THE CHANGING INSTITUTIONAL ROLE OF THE CONGREGATION

From a mediating institution among people and families in stable, stationary communities to an anchor institution for an increasingly mobile people who were leaving farms, towns, and cities for suburban territories, the dominant role of the congregation changed along with the culture. That the culture might "use" its institutions differently at different times is not easily discerned within one's own lifetime and experience. But importantly, this change in the cultural role of the congregation that happened within my own lifetime was only one shift among many such changes that have had an impact on both congregations and communities over time. The longer view of history suggests that congregations have had multiple roles and served very different purposes as the culture and the needs of the people have changed.

In an essay on the history of American congregations, religious historian E. Brooks Holifield identified a series of roles that congregations assumed within their changing communities.[3] What is central over time to all the roles is that the institution of the congregation has fundamentally served as a "primary extrafamilial form of community" for much of the American population, but in different organizational forms. Beginning with the colonial beginnings of America, Holifield's typology of congregations include the following.

THE COMPREHENSIVE CONGREGATION (1607–1789)

New England courts, as well as the Virginia Assembly enforced mandatory attendance laws throughout the colonial period in which congregations played a very central role for both the individual and the community. Commonly, there was only one congregation for each village, town, or county. Under such conditions, in highly stable communities, attendance at worship was greater than actual communicant membership. The comprehensive congregation served as a center of order and conformity for a whole geographical area and provided a platform for the most highly educated leaders in the community. These early congregations provided the only regular small-group gatherings for people of all ages in the community. As a locus of community cohesion, diversity was held at bay, uniform behavior and belief was enforced, and stability within families was supported. The comprehensive congregation was in tight relationship with the state, often depending on state financing while reciprocating by performing public responsibilities, such as keeping records of births and deaths and providing relief to the poor and homeless. Social divisions were maintained by seating men and women in separate sections while Africans and American Indians were segregated into their own separate spaces.

However, by the middle of the eighteenth century the population had grown, and even small towns had more than one congregation. As diversity became entrenched in communities, the role of congregations began to shift.

THE DEVOTIONAL CONGREGATION (1789–1870)

Congregations proliferated. In 1780, there were fewer than 3,000; by 1820, there were about 11,000; by 1860, there were about 54,000.[4] Once primarily Congregational, Quaker, or Episcopal, congregations were increasingly Methodist and Baptist, introducing more and more American democratic practices and beliefs. Congregations were also joined in their communities by a fast-growing array of other voluntary associations that competed with the congregation's functions of fellowship, charity, dissemination of information, and organized action. People led more segmented lives in the fast-growing towns and cities of the developing America, and congregations followed suit—each congregation drawing a much more segmented and self-selecting people for whom the congregation tailored its own primary purpose of worship. Along with Sunday services, prayer meetings were formed, Bible classes, Sunday schools, devotional gatherings, mission societies, and an array of small groups organized by age and gender.

Where the earlier comprehensive congregations included all people but observed social differences by seating people by social rank, the devotional congregations served more diverse and segmented communities by providing separate congregations for the wealthy and the poor, for persons of different origins, identities, and races. For example, one of the observable and enduring legacies of this period were towns with more than one congregation of the same denomination in which one of the congregations would serve the professionals, business leaders, and mill owners of the town, while the other congregation of the same denomination would primarily serve the workers and the laborers.

THE SOCIAL CONGREGATION (1870–1950)

The number of Catholics in America greatly increased with the arrival of immigrants from Ireland and Germany, so that by 1850, Roman Catholics were already a very large denomination within the country. Not able to count on other community institutions because of immigrant prejudice, Catholic congregations began to offer their members what was not available otherwise—relief societies, insurance societies, militia groups for discipline and entertainment, welfare and youth societies, temperance societies, and schools. Lutheran congregations provided similar services in communities with high levels of German, Swedish, and Norwegian immigrant settlement. Creating their own public order within the larger public order, the busy Catholic and Lutheran parishes raised questions among Protestants whose buildings remained quietly empty during the week between Sundays. The new busyness of the Catholic and Lutheran parishes foreshadowed the future of the American congregation.

Protestant congregations increasingly became the "social home" for its members, particularly in rural areas in which much of community life formed around the congregation. As Holifield pointed out, "One observer in 1890 spoke of 'a complete revolution' in the social life of American congregations, and the chief symbol of the change, he said, was the church parlor, which in any large church had often become 'almost as necessary as a pulpit.'"[5] Church socials and concerts, women's meetings, youth groups, girls' brigades, boys' brigades, sewing circles, benevolent societies, athletic clubs, and scout troops, were all part of the rapidly expanding social life of the congregation in its new role in the culture. This was particularly true in all immigrant communities where new arrivals searched for safe and supportive networks. In an increasingly busy and diverse culture, congregations had learned to exert their influence and values, as well as provide needed services, by dominating the activities of its members who were a segmented slice of the larger community.

This is where my story of sitting next to my grandfather Henry fits in. As a social home for multiple generations of families, the comprehensiveness of the congregation made it the base of stability for the larger community. At the same time, the congregation would manage its own changes as a bearer of tradition through the process of argument and accommodation.

PARTICIPATORY CONGREGATION (1950–1990)

The ideal of the social congregation as the center for worship along with a wide array of activities and services had a strong hold on American religion. But the once stable, family-centric communities in America began to give way to a much more mobile people who began to leave small towns in search of greater opportunities. It was during the post–World War II period that Gibson Winter offered his critique of the suburban captivity of the church as the American populace became much more mobile and educated following the war. Winter's criticism was that the congregation was increasingly becoming organizational. Congregations might feel the internal questioning of their clergy, who wondered if their congregations were simply becoming activity and entertainment centers in their community. But, as the mobility of the American people accelerated away from rural, small town, and urban areas into quickly expanding suburban outgrowths—new communities that people could move to but from which no one had previously come—new questions of belonging arose. Along with program activity, the organization and governance of the congregation became increasingly important. Clergy were interested in developing a sense of loyalty among the mobile populace, while laity were invested in developing a sense of belonging by having some "ownership" of the institutions they participated in. Offering more space for laity to participate in leadership and governance in their congregation served both interests. In earlier congregations, a leadership elite, usually clerical, defined the direction of the congregation. As the social congregation matured and the American populace became more mobile, lay groups and lay leaders took on a more democratic posture while their congregations pursued their role as a program center. This was simultaneously a period in which a flood of volunteer community organizations went through a significant growth spurt. Both the local congregations and a growing array of volunteer organizations such as Rotary, the Lions, Scouting, and Little League provided multiple places for a mobile people to settle in, claim ownership, and work for a better life. Holifield identified this impulse toward new forms of democratic participation as the hallmark of the congregation in the late twentieth century.

So, What Now?

I have drawn both heavily and directly from Holifield's essay in the above overview of the changing cultural roles of congregations through American history. It is important to see that congregations, like all established institutions, are not static constructions. Institutions have a primary purpose of carrying values and providing order, both in the lives of individuals (formation and behavior) and in the larger community (setting the terms for the common good). But the ways and means by which institutions satisfy that primary purpose morphs inventively over time as the context of culture ebbs and flows in its own ways.

Sensitive to such cultural and institutional changes, it is important to note that Holifield's essay was published in 1994, almost thirty years ago, and covers American history only up to the 1990s. As I seek to move this argument ahead, two things must be acknowledged. The first is that in Holifield's typology the role of the congregation is closely tied to, and responsive to, its cultural setting, which is dominated by the forces of history, demographics, technology, and the needs of the people. American culture did not stop changing in the 1990s. One can argue instead that the culture has continued to change in the last thirty years, certainly even more quickly and deeply than in prior decades. Given the close tie between the culture and the role of its institutions, including the institutional congregation, the steady stream of cultural challenges and changes over the past quarter of a century prompts questions about what the needed and appropriate role of institutional congregations in the American landscape is now.

This is a far different question from how established congregations are to be most effectively led, resourced, or helped in order to thrive in our own current cultural moment. Many of our present-day congregations are currently shaped around a role and relationship with their communities that was set in an earlier time and that is already tenuous and in question because of the changing culture. What is proposed here is the more challenging question of how institutional congregations (not necessarily their organizational forms) will fit on the still unfolding future American landscape and what role they will play in that future to address the needs of the people, while still advocating for the values that they hold. This is all yet to be seen, and the continual institutional anxiety about the preservation and resourcing of current organizational congregations will undoubtedly distract from the pursuit of this important question of future role and purpose.

As I hope to show, it will be increasingly necessary to differentiate between the *form and structure* of congregations as we now know them from the *role and function* that they will play in our changing culture with its shifting and unstable standards of values.

The second thing to be said is that the closer one lives to a time under study, the more difficult it is to see the larger cultural patterns that effect and influence the changes that people feel in their lives. For example, one might be clear that living in the midst of a global pandemic means to be caught in a massive time of cultural change, but, moving into a third year of this overwhelming pandemic-precipitated change, no one is able to be clearly predictive of what changes will finally come to our patterns of work, the education of our children, the practice of our arts, the mental health of separated people, or any of a host of practices and commitments that we once thought to be dependable and trustworthy. It is one thing to look over the long sweep of past and recorded history to be able to surface and understand observable patterns. It is a task of a different order to stand in the middle of swirling changes, such as those prompted by a pandemic, and to judge what is important from what is just notable, to identify what is a predictive pattern from what is just disruptive. Living in the midst of cultural change is one case in which being closer to one's subject allows one to see less, not more. This suggests that what comes next for the role of institutional congregations in our fast and continuously changing culture is still a matter of discovery, not prediction. However, what we can be sure of is that what we currently know about the form and structure of congregations is already in the process of being changed, so that congregations will be able to pick up the new role and purpose for which they are needed.

As noted above, Holifield makes the claim that across a history of changes in the roles that congregations have played, they have nonetheless retained a function as a primary extrafamilial form of community for much of the American population. In other words, whatever the role or the prominence of the congregation as a cultural institution, it has always been a "player"—always involved, always contributing to the lives of people and to the community. As an institution, the congregation has always been a participant in the culture. The role of participant is critically important and will be revisited in the final chapter of this book.

In the meantime, I will offer an argument in the next chapter that, as an American people, we are currently in the midst of a deep cultural shift in values. Since the 1950s, we have moved from a community-based culture (focused on the *we*) to an individual-based culture (focused on the *I*) beginning in the mid-1960s. The notion that we may be in the throes of a culture shift, back toward the values and the behavior of a *we*, community-based culture, is still an argument of discernment rather than an accomplished fact. But, for the moment, my purpose is to simply offer a snapshot of how institutions, such as congregations, participate in such cultural shifts. Historically, congregations have shifted their shape as the culture changed around them. This should prompt our curiosity about how congregations are now to change their form in this moment of our own deep cultural change.

Indeed, it is difficult to know at what level congregations participate in, contribute to, react to, or provide leadership for cultural changes. The relationship between institutions and cultural change is difficult to determine since deep cultural changes seem much more the sum of many, varied, often modest, and at first, seemingly unconnected modulations that accumulate until a major shift has happened. What can be said convincingly is that institutions do participate in culture and the changes that happen within that culture. Congregations do change with the culture and, perhaps, the reverse can be claimed as well—that the culture is also influenced to change by institutional congregations as they claim a new role in the lives of people and communities.

For example, in an essay on the Christian congregation as a religious community, theologian Langdon Gilkey captured the participation of the Protestant clergy and congregations in the cultural change that began in the mid-1960s. It is worth quoting at length because it paints a picture that many congregational leaders from that time would recognize.

Suddenly from somewhere new—or new on a wide scale—moral values became prominent, and older ones receded, especially among the student generation. "Make love not war" typified this shift, as did the sudden disgust with materialistic, nationalistic, and racist culture inherited from the recent American past (the musical Hair and the film The Graduate provide two examples) and above all the sudden dedication on the part of many students to the task of morally refashioning the world's social institutions. The more liberal elements of the clergy had long supported these new values and this sort of social action; many more now continued to do so. . . .

The Protestant church communities thus no longer represented and mediated a common set of "American" values. . . .

Almost without warning the leading segments of the churches did not so much represent the dominant establishment as embody an anti-cultural sectarian ethos; they saw themselves as alienated "advance units" committed to the revolutionary movements of liberation from the oppressive elements of the culture as a whole.[6]

As the congregation was being changed by the culture, so Gilkey offers a picture of the culture being changed by the congregation. This is a picture recognizable by a fair share of Protestant congregations and their leaders who pushed against the culture in an effort to shift toward more individual values of freedom rather than the established community values of conformity. To what degree congregations helped to create this change, participated in, or just reacted to this change that surrounded them is not the essential question here. What is to be argued is that congregations, like other institutions, are simultaneously part of, changed by, and instrumental to such cultural shifts—and in the process need to find their own new cultural location, role, and changing goals that would reflect their essential purpose.

Individuals can easily believe that the institutional form that they have personally experienced is an established norm and expect it to last over time, but, the larger view of history is that institutions, congregations included, are much more malleable, being formed and reformed continually even as they participate in and seek to change the culture around them.

MOVING FROM WHAT WE KNOW

So, what we have now is not clear. We are certainly in a culture that is not settled. In many ways, it is a world without coherence, without a reliable order—a subject to be taken up in the next chapter. Using the words of Robert Merton, Walter Brueggemann characterizes this as a time that is "a-nomos"—a time that is normless; a time of anomie.[7]

It is a time characterized by large contests over values. American populism stands against global neighborliness and interdependence. A resurgence of racism, white supremacy, and anti-immigration stand against advancements in equality, equity, and diversity. Efforts to curb climate change, which would benefit the full global community, butt up against national, regional, and corporate economic interests that disregard or deny those attempts. Such large contests of values have neighbors standing against one another over myriad issues, such as the importance of vaccines, the curriculum in public schools, the rights and conditions under which citizens may vote, and the role of guns in a staggering increase in the number of violent deaths. In this particular moment, we, as an American people, are not clear about who is a welcome part of our American fabric, how we will educate our children, who should make decisions, how we will manage our economy and national health, or even what behaviors are acceptable in order to live in community at the neighborhood level. We are a-nomos, without norms, without a reliable order.

It is in this climate of anomie that the question of the role of the institutional congregation is being raised. Older, established congregations (and their denominational organizations) are still able to live within the roles that once served an earlier culture, and they still function within the present religious landscape, but they serve a dwindling percentage of the population because of their allegiance to an earlier time. Their future will be short-lived if they remain as they are, choosing nostalgia over change.

Thus, a new question must be formed. Not a question of how we will care for and extend the life and service of the current form of the institutional congregation that is now under stress. The question needed is one that will help us to explore the role of the institutional congregation in a fast-changing culture that is, so far, without reliable form. The question that is needed is one that will help us to frame the central values and truths that the institutional congregation must align itself with for its next chapter in its very long history. The question needed now is one that allows us to look into an uncertain future without the burden of inherited assumptions of how congregations must be and behave. The leaders in the next stage of congregational history will need to address the question, "What now is a congregation?"

Given that the role and structure of the congregation is inextricably tied to the context of its surrounding culture, the next step then is to seek a deeper understanding of the cultural moment in which we live. It is to that deeper understanding that we now turn.

CHAPTER 3

Being at the End of Our Rope

Living in a World without a Reliable Order

WHAT IF WE ARE AT THE END OF OUR ROPE? THIS IS NOT A QUESTION of despair. It is rather straightforward. What if we've gone down a particular road, pursued a particular direction, followed a set of values—all with good intentions—but to a conclusion in which additional steps are a threat necessitating change?

It happens. Calling up the wit and wisdom of Anglican bishop, the Right Reverend Mark Dyer, Phyllis Tickle begins her analysis of the changes to Christianity with the observation that about every 500 years the church must have a giant rummage sale and rethink again what to keep and what to slough off—what is at its core and what must be scuttled—to make room for renewal and new growth.[1] Consider the 500-year progressions. About 500 years after the time of Jesus and the formation of Christianity came the dark ages and the fall of the Roman empire. In that time of deep turmoil, Pope Gregory I (540 CE) oversaw a time in which monasticism sought a way to preserve and protect the church, and the Council of Chalcedon found a way for the church to move ahead in its Roman, Greek, and oriental forms. At the next leap of 500 years, the church experienced the Great Schism (1054 CE) in which the Greek and Roman churches divided over the mass and the doctrine of the Holy Spirit. This was only to be followed about 500 years later in the Great Reformation (Martin Luther nailed his ninety-five theses on the Wittenberg gate on October 31, 1517 CE) splitting the Roman

Catholic and Protestant churches into their different forms. Take another 500-year step and we are in our own day in the twenty-first century.

It seems as if 500 years has been the limit for the global Christian Church to live with established norms, assumptions, agreements, and practices before the stress becomes so great that old ways die, giving space for the birth of new ways. So, are we now at the end of another rope? Have we pursued current values, assumptions, and practices to a logical end—suggesting that further steps along our current path without attending to necessary adjustments may have negative returns?

OUR CURRENT CULTURAL UNWINDING

If we can think this way about the church, we can also have a similar conversation about our culture being at the end of its current rope and needing a significant change of direction. Indeed, to understand the contemporary church at the end of its rope today requires an understanding of the parallel stress that is currently being lived out in a culture at the end of its rope. Consider the argument in chapter 2 that there is a direct link between a culture undergoing changes and the changes experienced in its institutions such as congregations.

What seems increasingly clear at this early point in the twenty-first century is that we are facing the death of an old epoch and the beginning of a new, yet undefined one. The language has been in our social literature for a while now as our academics and critical observers from multiple disciplines have written of a postsecular shift, of a postenlightenment time, of living in a postcapitalistic society, of being a postscience and postmodern people. It is easier to speak of what we are leaving and what is being left behind—such as our trust in science and institutions, our once complete and unquestioned dependence on uninterrupted progress, our sense of shared truths. It is harder to speak of where we are now heading, but we do seem to be in the midst of a deep cultural shift that will define our next years as the beginning of a new and different epoch.

Evidence of this cultural shift is being gathered and written about incessantly: a pandemic and postpandemic deep shift; a rising global populism spawning an historic political divide in the United States and elsewhere; a resurgence of white supremacy and racism; an economic divide between the wealthy and the poor that is eviscerating the middle class; a shift in who holds power and how it is wielded that is underwritten by changes in technology and communication; mercurial shifts in international agreements and relationships that undermine global stability and security; a climate change crisis that resides quietly beneath all other challenges with deadly global consequences . . . Such a sentence must end with an ellipse because it is incomplete. Indeed, each of us can add our own evidence and symptoms of cultural disruption from what seems to be an unending stream of changes. There is no trustable future because there is no surely formed present. We live in an unformed moment—"a-nomous."

Importantly, this unformed moment is further exacerbated by the speed of change driven by technology and social media. The description offered by Polish sociologist Zygmunt Bauman captures it well as a "liquid culture."[2] By liquid culture, Bauman means a world changing so quickly that the time necessary for a reasoned response is disallowed. By the time a response to any change is determined and moved toward implementation, the condition requiring the response will have yet changed again. How do we make sense of the deep changes that we now live in that come at us with such furious pace?

Given the depth of the change in our liquid culture, we are now at what William Strauss and Neil Howe call a "turning."[3] Cultures, like all living systems, balance their movement ahead in an oscillating pattern in which direction forward is managed by weaving a path back and forth between competing extremes. As cyclical historians, Strauss and Howe have documented this oscillating pattern in terms of a continual generational weaving among repeating value systems.

A familiar example on a small recognizable scale is child- rearing. Where one generation seeks to direct and control the development of their children through rules and constrained behavior, the next generation seeks to unleash the development of their children by unrestricting their behavior—only to be followed again by the next generation, which seeks once more to impose boundaries on their children's behavior. This oscillation between *constraint* and *freedom* in child-rearing styles is a natural way that generations have of steering to avoid the most negative aspects of either of the two poles of freedom and constraint. As Strauss and Howe note, each generation corrects the excesses of the generation that went before, while the next succeeding generation will then correct the excesses of that generation which went before it. This leads to a situation in which every generation naturally speaks poorly about the one that went before and the one that will come after. Nonetheless, the oscillating pattern of generational child-rearing styles provides a healthy cultural balance between the values of discipline and creativity, both of which are essential to the development of children.

Overlaying these more modest self-correcting "turnings" of generational practices and value systems that happen every nineteen to twenty-six years (the normative range of generational time), there are also oscillating patterns of much deeper, much longer, turnings in which whole cultures seemingly reverse their defining values. In the United States, the most recent reversal of fundamental values of our social contract began in the mid-1960s in which the constraining and relational values of the early twentieth century began a shift toward the liberating and individual values of the second half of the twentieth century.

THE SOCIAL CONTRACT

This shift can be seen in the way the American social contract changed. A social contract is an inherited, unwritten construct that shapes agreement on the relationship between the individual and the greater community. In other words, a social contract determines the way in which we agree to live with one another.

The early half of the twentieth century was marked by a social contract that Daniel Yankelovich described as a "giving/getting compact."[4] In order to get, one first needed to give. To have a happy marriage and family that would sustain one into old age, one first needed to give effort, faithfulness, resources, and attention to the people in the family. To provide for one's family's needs and to have a secure retirement in the future, one first needed to give steady and faithful work to one's employer. This early-twentieth-century giving/getting compact was *a relational social contract focused on the common good* in which one provided for the self by providing for the others. It was all about "we." And in that "we," the other was to come first.

Beginning with the tumult of the 1960s (which rose from the excessive accumulation of constraints that individuals felt from a cultural overfocus on "WE") the second half of the twentieth century saw a deep cultural turning of values toward a new social contract, this time focused on the individual. Hugh Heclo described this new social contract as a "moral polestar."[5] The terms of this new social contract state that every individual is free to pursue his or her own needs and pleasures, unhampered by others, up and to the limit of when their own pursuit infringes on the pursuit of other individuals for the same. No longer a relational contract, this new turning of cultural values produced *an individual contract*. This new individual moral polestar does not note connections among people but the boundaries and limits between people. Not about the common good and the "we," this is a social contract about the "I"—an "I" closely attended to by technology, social media, and consumerism.

Consider the historic turmoil of the "freedom generation" of the 1960s, the "me generation" of the 1970s, and the "greed generation" of the 1980s. These were all extensions of the influence of the individual-based moral polestar over the older, established common good giving/getting compact. The cultural vales were going through a "turning." Whatever nicknames are attributed or earned along the way, the transition between epochs is a wilderness experience, much like that of the Israelites leaving Egypt in search of new promises—of leaving excesses that begin to feel like slavery behind by moving toward countervailing alternatives in search of new freedom. What history teaches, however, is that such turnings also eventually lead to exposing a new set of excesses that will eventually need their own oscillating correction in the future.

Importantly, as we proceed through the 2020s, the unformed nature of a technology-driven global populism in a time of a pandemic is presenting just such another epochal shift in the deep cultural oscillation between competing value systems that all cultures use to find their way ahead. Both Chief Rabbi Jonathan Sacks[6] and sociologist Robert Putnam[7] argue that we are in the throes of another surge ahead—this time oscillating away from the extremes of practicing "I" values, pushing more strongly toward the countervailing "WE" values. From an individualistic consumer society with an "attention economy"[8] that both glorifies and monetizes the individual, we are once again beginning to reach out tentatively in search of the common good. Having experienced the excesses of an earlier focus on the "we" that reached its peak in the 1950s, our culture oscillated toward values and behaviors that by 2020 overly preferences individuals—the "I." Now, having experienced the excesses of over attention to individuality, we are oscillating forward once more in search of community—an expression of the "WE." At the end of its current rope, the North American culture is fitfully seeking a way ahead on a different path. How and whether our culture swings convincingly toward the common good of the "WE" is not yet conclusive.

OSCILLATIONS

It is important to recognize that coming to the end of one cycle of values is not hitting a proverbial wall. It may feel like a conundrum, but being at the end of our cultural rope is not at all the same as being at a dead-end. It is simply an antecedent moment to moving in a different, often opposing direction in order to move ahead. Much of life is lived within an oscillating cycle between the extremes of competing values or circumstances that are held in tension—between growth and recession, between equilibrium and disequilibrium. These cycles are natural rhythms that can be expressed as business cycles, news cycles, brainwaves, circadian biological rhythms, or oceanic El Niño Southern Oscillations. Once a rhythm moves too closely toward the extremes of one pole, there is a natural countermovement toward the alterative pole as described in figure 3.1.

This rhythm can even be expressed in our spiritual lives. Bruce Reed of the Grubb Institute offered a general theory of religion in which the individual naturally oscillates between a mode of self-dependence (intradependence), in which the person operates with a personal sense of wholeness and control, and a countervailing mode of dependence on God (extradependence), in which a sense of incompleteness and lack of control makes one reach beyond the self for strength.[9] It only makes sense. Being too self-dependent allows us to think that we hold all control and know all answers. To remain in this mode for too long is a slippery slope tilted toward disaster in a world beset by complexity and

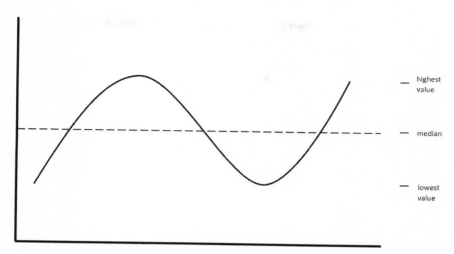

Figure 3.1. An Oscillating Cycle

mystery. So, the natural "correcting" human impulse is to reach out to God for strength, courage, and meaning making. However, to remain for too long fully dependent upon God makes the individual passive to the whims and changes of the world that we all live in, rather than participate as a functional partner with God in search of something far better. Life is well-lived as we seek the ever-changing balance between following our own passions and convictions, tempered and directed by spiritual practices that connect us to that which is beyond ourselves. Indeed, Reed describes how the act of worship invites us into the extradependent mode of recognizing our need for God on the Sabbath (regression), so that we can reassert the interdependent mode for the following week (reordering), participating in the world with purer motives and greater purpose. It is the covenant relationship in classic oscillating form. Reed graphed the relationship in figure 3.2.

AN OSCILLATING CULTURE

As a preeminent sociologist of the American experience, Robert Putnam makes his case in similar fashion, arguing that the American culture has come to a transition point in a long cycle of shifting cultural values and is primed to begin a new, countervailing direction—an oscillation of

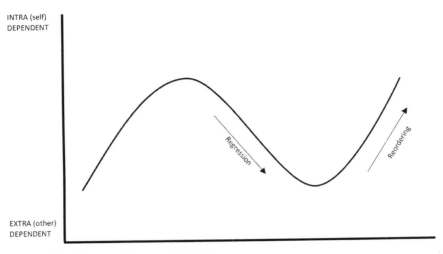

Figure 3.2. A General Theory of Religion

values. He points to the natural, reoccurring cyclical movement in values between a preference for the individual (an "I" culture) and the dominance of the common good (a "WE" culture). It is a repeating, cyclical oscillation of cultural cohesion determined by the attention we give to the opposing values of either "I" or "WE." The oscillation between these two sets of values manages the tension that Alex de Tocqueville noted in the 1830s in his observations about our democracy existing between "the twin ideals of freedom and equality; between respect for the individual and concern for the community."[10] Freedom reflects the desire of the individual, while equality is the ideal of people living together.

Understanding such cultural turnings requires a long view of history since the shifting of values and social contracts is a gradual process seemingly independent of daily or even annual changes. However, to see the longer cultural shifts it is often helpful to begin first with the short view of remembered history. Understandably, most of us can best relate to the period of history remembered in our own or our family's living history—a period of time that generally now covers the 1950s to the current time. The height of the values of the common good (the "WE" culture) was in the 1950s—a time of high community cohesion. Again, as noted in chapter 1, it was a time of national unity that kept some groups of people quietly sidelined. Nonetheless, it was a time in which differences were constrained and conformity enforced all in support of the common good—the "WE." Since that time there has been a strong cultural movement toward the values of the individual—a time of low community cohesion. If this change were to be graphed, it could be expressed as follows in figure 3.3.

The graph looks very much like a decline. In fact, it replicates the all-too-familiar graph that North American religious organizations have so closely tracked based on their own membership and participation data. In the case of my own United Methodist denomination, the peak year of 1965 was the last year that the denomination posted a net overall gain of membership. Since that time, the denomination has tracked, with great anxiety, a continual drain of membership, resources, and influence. Other mainline and evangelical Protestant denominations, the American Roman Catholic Church, and the Reformed and Conservative movements of Judaism (along with an overwhelming host of membership-based civic organizations) similarly tracked their own variation of the same organizational decline—all with shared anxiety over the weakening of their institution. The decline in community cohesion (the shift from "WE" to "I") found its parallel in the decline of all

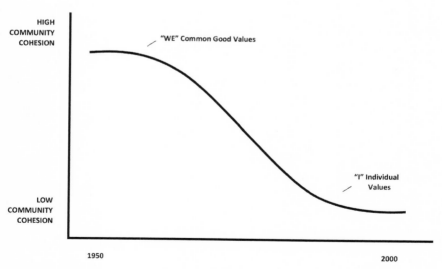

Figure 3.3. From Common to Individual Values

33

membership-based organizations. Cultures that measure low on community cohesion are not a supportive environment for institutions, especially for institutions in which participation is voluntary.

This similarity between the shift in values between "WE" to "I," and the graph of organizational decline in religious institutions is not arbitrarily imposed. One critical fact needed to understand the anxiety ridden organizational decline of so many religious and civic groups is that such membership-based organizations naturally thrive in common good, "WE"-based, cultural moments. It is not by accident that religious and civic groups were central to communities and to social networking in the 1950s. Subsequently, the following decades have not been kind to these organizations as the North American culture followed its cyclical path toward its counterbalancing preference of individual, "I," values. Community-based membership organizations do not live easily in "I"-centric cultures. More will be said of this in following chapters.

The second critical fact to note here is that a truncated review of the last decades tells a demonstrable story of institutional decline as noted above. However, were we to extend our review beyond the past 50 to 70 years to a period of the past 140 years—the longer view of history—what

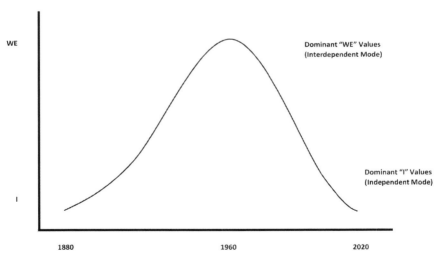

Figure 3.4. The "I–WE–I" Curve

at first appears to be a decline is more accurately a complete swing of social contract values in an oscillating cultural wave (see figure 3.4)

The contribution that Putnam brings to this conversation is that as a sociologist he has measured the changes in values, organizations, and behaviors using our own American data focused on economic, political, social, and cultural trends spanning 1895 to 2015. As Putnam writes,

> *By using advanced methods of data analysis to combine our four key metrics into a unified statistical story, we have been able to discern a single core phenomenon—one inverted U-curve that provides a scientifically validated summary of the past 125 years in America's story. This meta-trend [represented in figure 3.4] is a phenomenon we have come to call the "I–we–I" curve: a gradual climb into greater interdependence and cooperation, followed by a steep descent into greater independence and egoism.*[11]

Using his data to shape the interpretation of our national experience, Putnam identifies one cycle of a larger oscillating pattern. He begins his analysis showing how the 1870–1890 "Gilded Age" was remarkably similar to our own experience of 2000–2020. He tracks the eventual discomfort with the excessive individualism of the Gilded Age through the rise of the Progressive Era that followed in which, beginning in the 1920s, there was a great fanfare building toward the common man and the common good. The social contract was being reset into what we came to know as the giving/getting compact. But by the 1950s there began a discontent over the excessive and culturally enforced uniformity imposed on people that created the countervailing impulses for personal freedoms and expressions—the essential tension between the democratic ideals of freedom and equality earlier noted by de Tocqueville. The 1960s and the search for personal freedoms began as a move away from the dominant "WE" values and began to push the cultural pendulum toward the preference for the individual—the countervailing moral polestar social contract. Who would have guessed in the 1960s that "drugs, sex, and rock and roll" was itself a correction to an excess in the cultural values of community? Putnam uses our own national data to demonstrate this cultural oscillation between social contracts. For many of us, Putnam's analysis is a lens through which we can see and interpret our own life experience.

LIVING AT THE END OF A CYCLE

So, I will argue that we are living in an unformed moment because we are at the end of our rope, the end of a cycle. We have followed our values of individualism to excess, and there is nowhere left on this path to go that will be healthy and life sustaining.

"Every now and then," writes Ken Wilber, "evolution itself has to adjust course in light of new information on how its path is unfolding, and it starts . . . by making various moves that are, in effect, self-correcting evolutionary realignments."[12] Wilber devoted his life and work to "integral philosophy"—a discipline that seeks to integrate the various branches of human knowledge.[13] A "self-correcting evolutionary realignment" of our values and convictions is another description of a culture war—a contest with heated battles between competing values that, on the one hand are seeking dominance over the other, and on the other hand are seeking to balance the excesses of the other.

As we did earlier by using the smaller example of the oscillating values of freedom and constraint in child-rearing, it is helpful to break major shifts such as a culture war into smaller, more easily recognized examples. In this case, it may be helpful to look at the music used in worship—a major battlefield in recent decades in many congregations. The contest over church music has commonly been described as a generational difference in preference between hymnody (the preference of the older generations) and praise music (the preference of the younger generations). While the generational description of preferences generally holds true, the deeper significance is of a battle over music that reflects the larger cultural war over values and the social contract. Here, again, we can see evidence of the oscillating tension between the "I" and the "WE"—in Wilber's terms, a self-correcting evolutionary realignment of our cultural values.

A colleague, Len Kageler, Emeritus Professor of Youth and Family Studies at Nyack College, expresses the difference in musical hymnody not as hymnody versus praise music, but as the difference between horizontal and vertical songs.[14] Horizontal songs are songs sung as a group (as a "WE"), acknowledging the connection between singers. Vertical songs are sung as an individual (as an "I"), reflecting a sense of the single person standing before God.

Consider first an example of a horizontal "WE" song from a church hymnal, "God of Grace and God of Glory."

God of Grace and God of Glory,
on thy people pour thy power,
crown thine ancient church's story;
bring her bud to glorious flower.
Grant us wisdom, grant us courage,
for the facing of this hour.[15]

The words of this hymn were written by Harry Emerson Fosdick in 1930 as Americans were living in the tension between the Great Wars. The Gilded Age of individual wealth and excess was being challenged and brought to an end, the Great Depression was both a recent memory and a lingering reality, and it was a time when people turned to neighbor and community for strength. The culture was oscillating toward "WE." This hymn was a part of the standard hymnody of the church and an expression of the developing "WE" culture of that day. People were invited to stand side by side sharing common hymnals, all singing off the same page, following a four-part harmony in which every individual was responsible for their own part that, when brought together, would make up the whole. It was a horizontal experience in which people were to be aware of one another and of the group that they were a part of, and it was communal, asking God to "grant *us*," and reminding one another how *we* should be (wise and courageous) because of our faith in God. Horizontal hymnody brought people together to sing to one another as a way to rehearse a shared faith that the people held together. It was a "WE" experience.

Quite different, the vertical music, often described as "praise music" that expresses individual values can be seen in the example of the song

"You'll Come," released in 2008 by the Australian praise and worship group, Hillsong.

> Chains be broken
> Lives be healed
> Eyes be opened
> Christ is revealed
> I have decided
> I have resolved
> To wait upon You, Lord.

Written at the height of the "I" culture, this is not liturgical music meant to be sung to one another in a group but meant to be sung as an individual directly to Jesus as the humanly relatable expression of God. It is music to be sung in unison or alone, not in harmonic parts requiring others to make it complete. It is written in a singable range (one note over an octave) in the key of D, which is the optimal key for both men and women allowing everyone to sing individually with reasonable comfort. Commonly sung using lyrics posted visibly on overhead screens in a sanctuary, individuals are bound neither to a hymnal nor to a neighbor since there are no parts to blend and no need to be connected to the person standing alongside. Individual space can be used to raise arms toward God, or not; to rock rhythmically with the music or not. The focus is not on the "WE" that has gathered about the worshipper (the horizontal connection) but on the "I" connection between the individual and God (the vertical connection).

Great arguments were mounted by leaders in their congregations about which type of music was the right music to sing, and which generation of people in the congregation (past, present, or future) should be given preference in the music selected. The differences in the music felt pronounced, the generational preferences salient. What was much more subliminal was the way in which the choice of church music reflected the much larger contest of values that was going on in the culture.

Of course, it has been the values of individualism that have held the most recent sway in North American culture. Beginning in the 1960s, the sway toward individualism found its positive forms in the "civil rights movement, the worldwide environmental movement, drives for sustainability in business, the rise of personal and professional feminism, anti-hate legislation, a heightened sensitivity to any and all forms of social oppression of virtually any minority, and—centrally—both the understanding of the crucial role of 'context' in any knowledge claims and the desire to be as 'inclusive' as possible."[16] But, held too long and in too great prominence, the sway toward individualism capsized its own cherished values. The broadminded pluralism that made room for all individual differences slipped into a relativism that, Wilber notes, then collapsed into a nihilism. As a rejection of all group-based constraining religious and moral claims, nihilism became the moral philosophy of excessive individualism. Nihilism holds that no moral order can be drawn upon as authoritative over any other person or persons other than the individual who chooses to submit to its claims. Nothing in the world has real existence according to nihilism, which includes truth itself, since truth in a strictly individual culture must be malleable enough to conform to the experiences and needs of the individual. As we have experienced in politics, different truths do not even need to compete for "rightness." They simply need to present themselves as alternative truths allowing people to choose among them for the "reality" that best fits them and in which they would like to live.

If individualism, in its extreme, collapsed into a philosophical and political nihilism, Wilber argues that it also slid into an encompassing narcissism. There is only the self. Narcissism is a worldview (or at its extreme, a personality disorder) in which everything is understood as an extension of the self. There is no other, no community. A consumer-oriented society built on a digital technological base has learned how to "serve" the individual by making anything and everything available in support of the moral polestar. But beyond the individual's place in a consumer society, Jennie Odell has made the argument that we are now a part of an attention economy in which corporations have learned to monetize the very things that simply catch our attention.[17] As the adage now goes—if you receive something that you don't have to pay for (such as a podcast, a Facebook posting, a smartphone game app, a cell phone alert) you are not the consumer, you are the product. Someone has sold your attention to an advertiser or organizer, and the more that the marketer can prove that people are giving their attention to the message, the more the marketer can earn. That is to say, that in a hyperindividualistic culture, people have learned to build business models to provide revenue for anything that will capture a growing amount of the time and attention from the individual. The self is now a commodity.

There is an essential bankruptcy in the exclusive overfocus on the individual. Walter Brueggemann describes it as a timelessness: "When one is robbed of past and future, set in timelessness, when one is robbed of God and neighbor, there is only 'I' remaining. Then life becomes short and empty and barbarous."[18] As noted in chapter 2, the word that he gives to it is "a-nomos," a world without order; a world that is without norms. Pushed to its extreme—the furthest point along the path of individualism—there can only be the "I" and the "now." Norms, which are negotiated agreements among individuals in community, devolve into preferences, which are the nonnegotiable choices of the individual. Communities, which are gatherings of individuals with shared norms, devolve into tribes, which are gatherings of individuals who simply share similar individual preferences. At its extreme within the oscillation between the "I" and the "WE," the exclusive overfocus on the individual is a normless world. Again, as Brueggemann wrote, "A normless world is not a world for self-actualizing individuals. Rather, it is a jungle of competing, savage interests. We are at the edge of that in our culture, for the consensus has collapsed."[19]

We are, then, at the end of our cultural rope. The swing toward the individual that began in the 1950s–1960s has reached a point of anomie—a social instability that comes from a breakdown of communal standards and values. So, it is that white supremacy can contest anew with efforts of anti-racism and the Black Lives Matter movement. So, it is that the efforts of tribal "I"-ism can erupt in a 2021 attack on the Capital Building in Washington, DC, on January 6, 2021, as an outgoing president refused the election results, while only two weeks later on January 20, the new, incoming president stood at the same building for his inauguration, using the bipartisan language of "WE" in an effort to invite both red and blue states into a shared identity. In the oscillation between the identity and values of "I" and "WE," we have come to the end of the rope. It is a pivotal moment. There is clearly a contest afoot, and it is not yet settled which way we will go.

Pivotal moments, both in our private and our national lives, are frightening times. Quietly courageous people need to hold close to the understanding that coming to the end of a cultural rope is not, as mentioned, hitting a proverbial wall. It is rather the antecedent to moving in a different self-correcting direction in search of hope. As a nation we are now an "I" people who have lost our way. How else can we explain the denial of so many data-based realities such as climate change in which the interests of particular industries, corporations, and political leaders trump the shared need of all people for a viable, sustaining ecology, or, such as a global pandemic in which individual, so-called constitutional rights trump the shared need for widespread vaccination and the use of face masks to defeat a swiftly evolving, life-threatening virus, or, such as gun control in which individual second amendment rights can be manipulated by an NRA-controlled industry to ignore the needs of public safety and the experience of cities now tallying over 500 homicides by gun each year? As an "I" people, we have reached beyond any healthy limit of our own insistence on the importance of the individual in the face of our own data that increasingly tells us that we must find different ways to move ahead with agreement, cooperation, and an understanding of the common good.

To move the culture toward a more life-sustaining countervailing focus on the common good will require quietly courageous individuals willing to make both intuitive and data-based choices in favor of the "WE." A movement must begin at the individual and neighborhood level because of the gridlock currently built into the wider state and national decision-making systems. In this, quietly courageous individuals must understand, and not doubt or diminish, the power of their own intentions and actions. In the twelfth century, Rabbinic scholar Maimonides is to have said the following:

41

*One should see the world and see himself as a scale with an equal bal-
ance of good and evil. When he does one good deed the scale is tipped
to the good—and the world is saved. When he does one evil deed the
scale is tipped to the bad—and the world is destroyed.*

In this moment of a cultural turning, the individual choices of courageous
individuals can have a cultural, global significance in doing what whole
industries, governments, and nations cannot. It will take the effort of
these individuals, whom Margaret Wheatley calls the "Warriors of the
Spirit,"[20] to sustain the shift that is straining to tilt toward the common
good. It is time now for quietly courageous individuals to tip the scales
toward the common good by giving attention and support to the needs
of equality, community, and neighbor.

But equally, we will need to rebuild our institutions at the neighborhood level as platforms undergirding the shift to the common good.
It really is time for the church to speak again, and it need only be loud
enough for the people living next door to hear.

It is here that the question of "what now is a congregation?" from the
previous chapter fits in. Surely individuals will need to actively choose
which values and what truths they will use to guide their lives, their relationships, and their participation in the larger community, and, as noted,
those values and truths from which they can choose are in great contest
at this moment. However, individuals have always depended upon institutions to help them hold, shape, and practice the values, the disciplines,
and the behaviors that are most important to their lives and the world
that they understand themselves to be a part of. In the contest over the
oscillating values of "I" and "WE" in which we are currently caught, people will necessarily look to and depend upon institutions to affirm, shape,
support, and sustain their new choices of values and social contracts as
they seek to find their place in a very fast changing culture. If change
will first come from individuals making personal choices about what is
most important, those individual choices will need to be formalized and
advocated through institutional forms in order to be rooted in and thrive
in the larger culture. This is the heart of the question of what, now, is a
congregation.

So, it is that we need to more deeply understand how institutions hold and express values and how they offer disciplines of behavior appropriate to both their purpose and the needs of the larger culture. We need to understand how institutions work. It is to this view of institutions that we now turn our attention.

Chapter 4

Usufruct and Obedience to the Unenforceable

The Importance of Institutions

INSTITUTIONS SHAPE OUR LIVES. I GREW UP IN A METHODIST CHURCH with the biblical text of 2 Timothy 2:15 carved in embossed gold letters above the altar: "Study to show thyself approved unto God." It came from one of Paul's pastoral epistles to his associate, Timothy. It is, if you will, from one of the lesser texts of the New Testament. No one ever specifically pointed to or spoke to me about this golden text that was so central to my family's worship space as I was growing up. I don't remember our pastors ever preaching about this text. It was just there, silent.

Yet, I remember it. I remember it word for word in its King James form. It still appears in my mind's eye as golden letters carved into dark oak wood above the altar in a sanctuary that I haven't visited in over four decades. It could be said that it was a life lesson that traveled with me and has contributed to who I am. No doubt it traveled with me because it was so companionable with other life lessons I learned about worthiness, responsibility, and attention to work. It certainly fit with the family in which I grew up where study and work were clear priorities for our attention. One of my recurrent flippancies meant as self-deprecating humor is that I am part English, part German, and part Methodist—therefore I've never been late to a meeting in my life! If 2 Timothy was silent in my growing up, it certainly left its mark.

45

The fuller text is this: "Study to show thyself approved unto God, a worthy workman that needeth not to be ashamed." Being a worthy worker is of high value in my life, taught by my parents (the institution of family), part of the backbone of my faith (the institution of the church), and for which I have been commonly rewarded by the institutions of education, and those connected to employment, and community.

For me, the lesson from the embossed altar in a church is *usufruct*—something that is a fruit from the past, that constrains or directs me in the present in a good and healthy way, and that I would do well to pass on to the future. In his work on institutions, Hugh Heclo points out that the word usufruct is a venerable legal term traceable to pre-Christian Roman law. "It refers to the right to make full use of something while also being under the obligation to pass on intact, without injury, the substance of the thing itself."[1] Usufruct is what institutions do. They hold essential values received from the past, encourage the use of those values in the present, and extend those values to the future. I am helped by Heclo's connection of usufruct to institutions, and I shall continue to draw heavily on his insights in this discussion about institutions.

First, my argument has been that, as institutions, congregations have been far from static in form and practice over the time of our American history and that the role they assume in their communities and in the lives of their adherents continually changes to fit the cultural moment in which they exist. Second, I argue that if congregations conform to the needs of their surrounding culture, their religious leaders certainly need to pay attention to the fact that our own culture is at a "turning." Ours is a moment of cultural turmoil in which values and truths are contested by tribal subcultures and in which we are not yet sure about where we as a nation or as communities of faith will next head. Certainly, our congregations, as much as they are institutional expressions of faith, are also caught up in this cultural contest. We cannot ignore that because of the current national political polarization these congregations might lean closer to political positions than to biblical principles at times. And, while some congregations might now be coopted into the role of partisan participant in a culture war, that certainly is not the role needed from our religious institutions for the future. Ours is a chaotic moment, and our religious institutions can certainly be caught up in that chaos. But something different, something more, is trying to be birthed. The unsettledness of our day should not prompt congregations to take sides in a partisan cultural war but bring forth the countercultural truth that they hold in service to our time of tumult. There will be more about this in the next chapter.

The oscillating nature of both history and of living systems suggests that as an American people we are beginning to push back against (subversive resistance to) our current excess of attention to the individual values of "I" that have now overexpressed the importance of individual freedoms, the personal pursuit of wealth and power, and truth dependent on the preference and pleasure of the self. There is beginning to be pressure in our American culture seeking to sway, with a countering force, back toward a new understanding of the common good. The future is far from determined, but there is little doubt that we are at a turning.

It is this undetermined cultural moment that allows leaders to form new questions about what the congregation, as an institution of faith, will be in the future as the turning reshapes our culture.

As noted, leaders of congregations have most recently been overly anxious about the organizational viability of their institution. Beginning in the 1960s, the individual culture of the "I" has not been kind to congregations and to all other membership-based organizations. The anxiety of leaders has been focused for decades on addressing problems of cultural fit, adequate resources, and the development of strategies to capture as much "market share" of adherents as possible. Nonetheless, within this anxiety there is a cohort of those who are building a quieter, more resolute conversation that seeks to look differently at the future. This resolute conversation is shaping around questions concerning the purpose of institutional congregations, concerning the core and essential truths held by institutional congregations, and concerning how institutional congregations will now live with their purpose and their truths in a quickly changing culture. What role will congregations *now* play in a turning culture?

To move closer to addressing such new and critical questions, leaders will need a deeper understanding of institutions themselves.

47

UNDERSTANDING THE IMPORTANCE OF INSTITUTIONS

While there may be multiple ways to look at institutions, in his work, Heclo locates a central point of agreement among experts: "institutions have to do with creating and enforcing rules."[2] This central function of institutions is the basic tool of usufruct and sheds light on the current cultural discomfort with institutions and with their countercultural position. The moral polestar of the present American social contract, as noted earlier, is the freedom of the individual to pursue his or her own needs and pleasures, unhampered by others, up and to the limit of when his or her own pursuit infringes on the right of others for the same. Rules, by their very nature, hamper that individual pursuit embedded in the current social contract. In an individual culture, rules (and therefore institutions) are experienced as constraints.

But what if rules are not constraint but formation? The rules that we encounter from healthy institutions are how we are formed. Engaging these institutions and their values are how we give shape to our lives. This is the usufruct of 2 Timothy contributing to my understanding of personal responsibility as I grew up. However, the rules of institutions form not just the individual but form communities as well by shaping how those individuals will live together with one another. When these values, rules, and practices of institutions shape a larger consensus in the culture, they become guidelines and disciplines for how we best live together in community. This is the antithesis of, and antidote to, a-nomos. As noted, in times of greater community cohesion the guidelines and disciplines of institutions lean more toward the common good. Without these rules provided and supported through institutions, we are ill formed as individuals, and we live poorly in community.

The Ten Commandments as Institutional Usufruct

Consider something as basic as the Ten Commandments, bedrock teaching of the institutional church. This is certainly usufruct—truth received from the past, to be practiced in the present, and certainly needed for the future.

There are those who might argue that these core commandments are, most importantly, a moral code for the individual that determine a path to personal salvation. Obey these rules completely and heaven is guaranteed—break one or more and hell awaits. But this sense of personal salvation connected to an other-worldly heaven and hell is a product of the fourth-century understanding of the universe and the effort of ancient people to make sense of the tension between good and evil within themselves.

More to the point, the context of the Ten Commandments offers a different understanding than an interpretation of personal salvation. The story of the Exodus is not a personal story but a communal one. In the Exodus, God did not make discrete and individual covenants with each individual in the community but with all of Israel. As the ancient rabbis taught about Moses' encounter with God on Mt. Sinai, "When God revealed himself to Israel, the world fell silent, because this moment was pivotal not only to Israel but to all Creation."[3] This was a covenant, not with individuals but with a whole people—with all of creation. Israel, at the time of the delivery of the Ten Commandments, was in a difficult (unformed, chaotic) time in a way that reflects our own. The Israelites were escaped slaves in an unknown wilderness with unsure leaders. They had questions about the basics, even about their supply of food and water, and they were not even sure of what direction to travel to escape the wilderness. Any known, usual, or dependable norm of daily routine, such as when to get up, where to work, and what to do, was gone.

How then do a people in such chaos reorder and reorganize themselves when all constants, constraints, and directions have been removed? The Ten Commandments provide the basic reordering inscribed on two tablets, five commandments on each.[4] The rabbinic teachers point out that the first tablet contained laws regarding the people's relationship with God. Much of what was on the first tablet has to do with remembering and honoring. This was to put the people in right relationship to the often-unseen or unrecognized reality—that God, not Pharaoh or any other temporal agency, is to be remembered as the Creator, and that they are under God's promise and direction. This was the alternative narrative to the prevailing narrative that they held, which was one that was fearful of Pharaoh's pursuit and afraid of the inhospitable wilderness ahead. More will be said later of the necessary alternative narrative of faith later, but on this first tablet was the reminder of the identity of the Israelites as a people living under the covenant and care of God. This was instruction on how to be with God.

The second tablet held commandments that reordered relationships among the people themselves. Here was the reorganization of how the people were to live with one another. This was instruction on how to be with one another. The rabbinic teachers point out that the Ten Commandments in Exodus 20 are followed immediately by the civil law in Exodus 21. "The juxtaposition of this Sidrah (dealing primarily with civil and tort law) with the Ten Commandments and the laws of the Altar provide a startling insight into Judaism. To God there is no realm of 'religion' in the colloquial sense of the world."[5] Life is to be ordered in all of one piece, religious and secular, woven together with great attention to how to be in community with one another. Rules of understanding (how we are to see the world) and rules of behavior (how we are to be in the world) are necessary in order to weave together a full creation. This is formation at its most essential core.

To these people in a wilderness desert, the Ten Commandments were not a code for personal salvation but the institutional rules of a full covenant community needing to restructure and re-form itself. If an Israelite wanted to get through the wilderness as fully human, then here were ten essential rules of faithful living that would sustain him or her. If the Israelites together hoped to be a people—to be a healthy, viable, community—here were values and disciplines that would sustain them in their shared experience. Here were rules of living that would form the ancient Israelites in ways that would provide for a future. For us they are usufruct—rules inherited from the past, needed in the present, and to be passed on to the future because of their universal truth and importance.

Rules are good. They are necessary. For there are always the tendency and temptation for people to choose how to live unwisely. As Heclo notes, "Precisely because men [and women] are not angels, we turn to institutions and their standards to help restrain and channel our ordinary human impulses to lie, cheat, and steal (among other numerous faults that come naturally to our species.)"[6]

Three Basic Systems of Institutions

So, it is that we need institutions to form us as individuals and to form us into healthy communities. In their most basic forms, Jonathan Sacks points out that all countries and cultures have three basic systems of institutions.

> *There is the economy, which is about the creation and distribution of wealth. There is the state, which is about the legitimization and distribution of power. And there is the moral system, which is the voice of society within the self; the "We" within the "I"; the common good that limits and directs our pursuit of private gain. It is the voice that says No to the individual "Me" for the sake of the collective "Us."* [7]

There are multiple organizations within the domains of each of these institutional systems through which their rules are determined and enforced. We tend to conflate the idea of an institution and the organization or organizations connected to it—a distinction that will be taken up shortly. For the moment, staying close to the important insight that Sacks offers, each of the basic forms of institutions of economy, state, and morality have multiple organizations in their service. Banks, markets, investment firms, mortgage companies, and credit unions are all organizations in service to the institutional system of the economy. Executive, legislative, and judicial organizations within their respective branches of government all serve the institutional system of the state. Congregations, mission agencies, voluntary association organizations, and many non-profit organizations serve the institutional system of morality.

Keeping sharp the distinction of the three basic systems of institutions allows for some helpful observations descriptive of our current cultural experience. For example, two of these institutional systems—the economy and the state—are arenas for competition in our culture. The economy and the state are dominated and governed by rules of winning and losing, of advantage and disadvantage, of permission given and permission denied. It is the third institutional system, that of morality, which is the arena of cooperation. It is to this institutional system of morality to which the common good belongs.

The distinction between where the values of competition and the values of cooperation are held is important when considering the oscillating turnings of cultural preferences over time. The argument offered here is that we currently live in an overexpression of the values of the individual, the "I," which is where the values of competition thrive. Each "I" naturally seeks their personal moral polestar in competition and contest with other "I's." As Wilber noted in the previous chapter, this overexpression has now brought us to the dead ends of nihilism and narcissism. Individualism favors competition over cooperation. It is not inconsequential that we are currently living in the age of celebrity. Celebrities are individuals celebrated for winning by being unconstrained by limits on behaviors, wealth, power, and attention that are more commonly accepted by or imposed on others. Using the work of Sir John Glubb on the decline of civilizations, Margaret Wheatley argues that our current rise of the celebrity culture in the United States is evidence of a final stage of culture in need of a new direction.[8]

Importantly, Sacks notes that in the age of the "I" (i.e., in celebrity cultures), the rules and constraints of morality are diminished. Sacks writes of morality "outsourced" to the other systems of the economy and the state.[9] What results is a diminished effectiveness of social constraints. For example, moral behavior around issues of racism, hate speech, and bullying is outsourced to the jurisdiction of the courts because there are few shared community moral sanctions now perceived against such behavior. Without a clearly expressed moral consensus that come from the organizations of the institutional moral system such as families, congregations and schools, rules around the practice of racism, hate speech, and bullying are outsourced to the state. Bullying becomes a matter of law in order to bring it under constraint. Abortion, likewise, falls under the jurisdiction of the state because conflicting personal moral decisions are forced into a competition of winning and losing by those unwilling to cede legitimacy to those who do not agree with their own position. Poverty and homelessness present issues to be resolved by the economy, government legislation and the courts, not by community expressions of empathy, equity, and care. Outsourcing morality to systems of power and competition results in an unsafe and weakened shared communal life.

Giving definition and enforcement of moral behavior over to the law invites people to push boundaries to the edge of the law or beyond for personal advantage. Morality deferred to the institutions of the state and the economy does not invite thoughtful compliance for the purpose of a larger good. When morality is outsourced, the institutions of morality such as marriage, family, and community, as Sacks notes, all atrophy.[10] As a carrier of the values of the institutional system of morality it is of little wonder that congregations and other forms of religious organizations have also atrophied. Heclo very descriptively wrote that "to live in a culture that turns its back on institutions is equivalent to trying to live in a physical body without its skeleton or hoping to use a language but not its grammar."[11] Having outsourced morality to other institutional systems, and having accepted the atrophy of our religious organizations, we are now a people seeking to live with something missing. And that which is missing exacts a cost. Sacks writes:

> So, our current individualism is liberating. We are free as never before to be as we wish and live as we choose. . . . We can do things of which our ancestors could hardly dream, but what they found simple we find extremely hard. Getting married. Staying married. Being part of a community. Having a strong sense of identity. Feeling continuity with the past before we were born and the future after we are no longer here.[12]

What is missing is not easily obvious. It can be as simple, and as difficult to point to, as "manners." In his 1995 commencement address to Boston University, President John Silber decried the deterioration of civic morality and turned to the work of Sir John Fletcher Moulton, a much earlier English Jurist.[13] Moulton divided human action into three domains as can be seen below in figure 4.1.

The first is the domain of law in which people's actions are prescribed by law and must be obeyed. The third domain is that of free choice, which includes all those areas and actions in which the individual can claim complete freedom, unhampered and unrestricted. It is that which is in the middle, the second domain, which is less obvious but deeply damaging

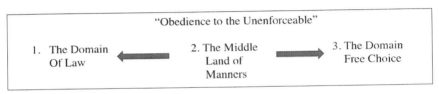

Figure 4.1. Sir John Fletcher Moulton

when missing. Moulton called this second domain "the middle land of Manners," which demands obedience to the unenforceable. Here a person's actions are not determined by law, but neither is the person free to behave without attention to, as Silber noted, "a sense of what is required by public spirit, to 'good form' appropriate in a given situation." Obedience to the unenforceable—the domain of the institutions of morality. This is the argument offered by Yale law professor Stephen Carter in his book *Civility: Manners, Morals, and the Etiquette of Democracy.*[14] Importantly, Carter argues that civility, the difficult to point to manners of a civilized people, is a value that ebbs and flows with a changing culture. It is an oscillating value that is strongest in cultural times of cohesion (the "WE" culture) and most missing in the times of "I" when cohesion gives way to personal and tribal competitions. But that which is missing exacts a cost. It is like a body without all if its bones, like speaking a language without using the rules of grammar that give structure, coherence, and meaning. It is living without the constraint and support that gives form and stability to the individual and the community.

What Do We Seek to Restore? Institutions and Organizations

What is missing in the chaos of our current cultural turning that causes us to feel like a body without all of its bones is our "institutions," which is not the same as our "organizations." Here we need to come back to take up an earlier distinction that was made very quickly. One of the hardest won insights for me over the past years is that:

Institutions are not organizations that house values, practices, and disciplines. Institutions are values, practices, and disciplines that often need and use organizations to bring their treasures to the people.

This is a critical and essential distinction that will allow us to move into the future aware of the treasure of our values that we must carry forward without being unduly hampered by organizational forms that no longer fit well with the fast-changing culture. Currently, many of our religious leaders are deeply focused on saving our organizations, when what is truly at risk is our institutions.

Remember that institutions are essential to our personal and communal lives—as the place where we hold our most precious values and where we establish and direct the behaviors and disciplines that will express and protect those values. Remember also that it is the institutions of our system of morality that we have allowed to atrophy by outsourcing their wisdom to the other competitive institutional systems of the state and the economy. To fully understand our institutions of morality and their values it is necessary to distinguish between the form and structure of an institution, in comparison to the purpose and the values of the institution. This is the difference between thinking of an institution as an *organization* (its form) and thinking of an institution as a *construction of social reality* (its function)—a distinction made by Heclo in his work on understanding institutions.[15]

As an organization, an institution is the ordering of the people, resources, and goals necessary for expected performance in alignment with particular goals. This is the basic work of all organizations. It is the institution as buildings, budgets, staff, departments, agendas, outputs, and resources. This is *how* we do institutions. It is attention given to the resources and activities of institutional organizations. Stabilizing and resourcing this organizational side of our institutions has been the focus of our anxiety about institutions over the past half century.

But as a construction of social reality, an institution is the infusion of value, purpose, and discipline into the arena of shared living in community. This is the *why* of institutions as they bring shape to who we can be as individuals at our best and how we can best live with one another. As a construction of social reality, an institution can be understood as a mental abstraction.[16] *It is attention given to a way of thinking, which leads to a way of behaving.* Importantly, it is a *consensual* mental abstraction in which there is widespread agreement on a way of thinking and a way of

55

behaving. As Heclo wrote, "institutions represent inheritances of valued purpose with attendant rules and moral obligations."[17] Institutions are a way of thinking and behaving with a moral purpose that is inherited from the past, to be used to structure a healthy present, to be passed on to the future. What institutions do is usufruct. It is so much more than organizations with budgets, mission statements, staff, resources, and goals. Yet, quite naturally we too easily think of institutions as organizations because their organizational form is the most common way in which we encounter them.

To be clearer about an institution as a construction of a social reality, it is helpful to look at an example of an institution that exists without an organizational form. Consider "the institution of marriage," an expression commonly used to identify a system of values and disciplines brought together to create a communal reality—a respectful, healthy way for couples to be and to behave for personal and social benefit. The institution of marriage speaks of covenant and commitment, personal fidelity and responsibility, public recognition of boundaries with community support, and a nurturing family environment to support the individuals who participate in the institution. Free of the *how* of budgets, structures, agendas, and organizational matters, the institution of marriage nonetheless carries the *why* of living in a particular way through an expression of values and disciplines of behavior. Also note that in the individual "I"-based culture of the past decades the rules and disciplines of the institution of marriage are experienced as a constraint on the individual resulting in a weakened consensus on this institution as a necessary construction of social reality. Burton points out that the lack of trust in the institutions of heterosexual marriage and in the church, which is the agent of the institution of marriage, have led millennials to marry later in life and to be three times as likely to never marry than their grandparents' generation.[18]

Nonetheless, the example of the institution of marriage helps to see that it is specifically the *why* of institutions, the construction of a social reality, that is the pearl of great price to be protected and to be carried into the future by institutional organizations, including the organizational church. Such *whys* of institutions are the treasure so deeply needed and sought after in our turning culture that must be carried forward even as we struggle with the *how* of institutional life that will need to radically change to accommodate the liquid culture, unwinding, great turning that we have entered. The *how* of our institutional religious lives—the organizational and programmatic shape of our congregations—is in flux once again, and we are currently without a clear sense of their changing role in a turning culture. This, after all, is the lesson of the changing roles of congregations in chapter 2, which began in the 1600s and is now dramatically different because of the progressive and multiple adaptations congregations have made over time to a constantly changing culture. This is why we must take seriously the question of what, now, is a congregation. Unless we are willing to be open and malleable about the how of the congregation, we may hamper the why which is now so deeply needed.

What remains constant is the fundamental recognition that the absence of institutions as constructions of reality is unthinkable for our future. Without them we are left only with the self, the individual. And, as noted in chapter 3, left unchecked to the point of excess it has been the primacy of the individual and the attending priority given to personal freedoms and individual rights that has led us to our current state of nihilism and narcissism and our absence of community. We may not currently trust or respect our present organizational institutions—an issue to be addressed below—but losing the treasure of our institutional constructs of reality because of our dissatisfaction with the clay pot of our institutional organizations is not a livable option.

To see more clearly the critical importance of our institutions as a way of thinking and behaving, consider an editorial column from David Brooks who wrote about propositional knowledge as one of the forms of knowledge that provides a reservoir on which our nation can thrive.[19] His topic was truth and how truth can be destroyed in national conversation. Propositional knowledge, Brooks notes, is acquired through reason, logical proof, and tight analysis. Distinct from lesser forms of knowledge such as political narratives, spin, news bites, and "alternative facts," propositional knowledge must be established by carefully using evidence. Importantly for our consideration Brooks points out that the acquisition of this kind of knowledge is a collective process of a "network of institutions [i.e., organizations]—universities, courts, publishers, professional societies, media outlets—that have set up an interlocking set of procedures [i.e., values and disciplines] to hunt for error, weigh evidence and determine which propositions pass muster." In other words, the great value of these institutions is not their organizational structure that provides form and stability, but their adherence to and advancement of their values and disciplines which provide meaning. The organizations exist in their service to the values.

This same distinction between the "why" and the "how" can be seen in other institutions, such as democracy and the scientific method. In the institution of democracy, there are multiple organizations brought together to serve a consensual agreement of how to be governed. The consensual agreement and practice of a way of thinking and behaviors practiced across those organizations, networks, professions, and practitioners is what brings life and influence to the institution of democracy. Likewise, in the institution of the scientific method, there are a host of organizations and individuals who agree to practice their science in a particular and exacting way so that discoveries can be tested, replicated, and trusted. Without the strong and faithful organizational "hows," the "whys" of our institutions falter and fail.

Brian Doyle makes this distinction between the how and the why in a much more poetic and personal way as a Roman Catholic. He wrote, "I saw for the first time in my life that there were two Catholic churches, one a noun and the other a verb, one a corporation and the other a wild idea held in the hearts of millions of people who are utterly uninterested in authority and power and rules and regulations, and very interested indeed in finding ways to walk through the bruises of life with grace and humility."[20] The difference between the how and the why. Imagine how sterile an organization of morality becomes when it overfocuses on its "how" and forgets its "why." Denominations, dioceses, conferences, congregations, universities, courts, publishers, and so on, all will undoubtedly need to recognize the instability of their current organizational forms under the pressure of technology, national and global realignments, and a liquid culture. They will need the courage to find their next organizational forms in our current cultural turning. But undimmed and unchanged are their whys, with which they must move forward with their capacity to shape consensual constructions of social reality that will make this cultural turning livable.

The Issue of Trust

If in our current cultural turning, we are to move closer to the common good—if we are to strengthen our tentative oscillation away from an over attention to the "I"—we will need to do more than reorganize and better resource our current institutional organizations. There will be two central issues to address.

The first is the discovery of the organizational forms and roles that our institutional organizations of the moral system will next need to inhabit. This is the challenge of the new question, "What now is a congregation?" This question is needed to explore what role congregations will *now* play in a turning culture. This is the long-term question under inquiry in this writing to which we will continually return. While there is much, and continually increasing experimentation in this area, we are far from holding any conclusions because of the churning of our present cultural chaos.

The second issue is more immediate and short-term, requiring as much direct attention as possible. This is the issue of institutional trust. It is a trust that has evaporated. As argued, institutions are more than a good idea; they are essential to our personal and communal lives. Institutions are where we hold our most precious values and the way in which we establish and direct the behaviors and practices that will express and protect those precious values. We depend on institutions for our own personal formation and for the formation and protection of community—the "common good" writ both large (nationally) and small (neighborly). Despite this critical importance, institutions of all stripes (e.g., government, military, politics, religion, health care, education, finance, athletics) have suffered in reputation and acceptance during the "I"-based culture of the second half of the twentieth century. The present disrespect of institutions is important to understand if they are to be a part of what must be carried into the future.

There are three notable causes of the current diminishment and mis-trust of institutions. The first two come from the critical work that Heclo did on understanding institutions.[21]

1. Institutions are not trusted because they have earned our mistrust. Politicians who misrepresent truth in order to garner personal or party power; church systems that subject children to pedophile clerics; financial systems that sell worthless financial instruments to uninformed investors for corporate gain; banks that package risky mortgages and encourage them onto homeowners who don't understand and can't afford them; for-profit prison systems that reward investors by overfilling cells with minority populations. We can all be quick with examples of institutions that have earned our personal mistrust.

   However, the level of institutional mistrust goes well beyond our own personal experience and has grown to the level of full genera-tional learnings about the untrustworthiness of the very institutions that are to be depended upon for ordering life. Looking only at our political institutions (the organizations of our institutional system of the state), Heclo offers what he calls "A Baby Boomer's Primer for Political Distrust."[22] For five full pages in his book he lists only the most high-profile political events of mistrust, beginning with the resignation of President Eisenhower's chief of staff, Sherman Adams, in 1958 for illegal acts in office to the 1999 impeachment of President Clinton for perjury and obstruction of justice. Along the way in this five-page tabulation are over forty nationally profiled reasons for mistrusting governmental leaders and organizations. These (and more) institutional improprieties are recognizable to all baby boomers. And consider that this list ends in 1999, leaving more than an additional two decades of political examples of mis-trust that have continued to undermine our institutional system of the state. To our great diminishment other institutional systems of religion, health, science, and more have their own parallel histories of improprieties.

If institutional systems are the expression of structure and means of our lives together—the common good—then the abuse of these institutional organizations for personal power and gain, and the untrustworthiness of these institutional organizations to serve the common good may have well contributed to the cultural oscillation toward the primacy of the individual beginning in the 1950s–1960s. If that which is to serve the common good cannot be trusted, and if individuals can so easily harness organizations of the common good for personal gain, it stands to reason that the people will shift toward personal empowerment and individual competition. It explains why greed can replace generosity as a cultural value. Our institutions are not trusted because the individuals leading those institutions have blatantly misused them, earning our deep mistrust.

2. Our mistrust, however, goes beyond that which was earned by misdeed. Even at their best, institutions are diminished because they are now experienced as the enemy of individual fulfillment, as has been noted earlier. As the carriers and enforcer of rules it is the nature and design of institutions to advocate disciplines or practices—limits and boundaries to the immediate pleasures and preferences that we might seek as individuals. Picking up the earlier conversation, the imposition of disciplined practices and limits is not naturally welcomed by an "I" culture that follows the moral polestar of the individual as its social contract. If the dominant cultural consensus encourages the individual to pursue immediate needs and pleasures, then institutional constraints to that pursuit will feel unwelcome and untrusted since they defer immediate pleasures to a later time or for a larger good. For example, the institutional direction for an individual to set aside a portion of current earnings in a 401K for much later use in retirement is perceived by many in the individual culture more as an imposition than as responsible advice that will serve and protect both the individual and the common good. In such ways the practices of institutions are simply perceived to be out of step with the current values of the culture at the moment. It

is not surprising that employees reject retirement savings programs as constraints on their current spending, even while being aware that such retirement programs are for their own long-term benefit.

Keep in mind that the rules of retirement programs such as a 401K are explicitly set out and easily accessed in the documents of the financial organizations that offer and manage them. To choose against using them is a conscious choice. But recall Sack's earlier observation that even behaviors earlier felt to be simple disciplines such as getting married, staying married, and being part of community are much more difficult because they are experienced as personal constraints rather than conditions of shared stability. The rules and practices of marriage and community are much less obvious than the explicit contracts of a 401K. Nonetheless, they are felt as an imposition and constraint on the freedom of the individual. In the oscillating contest between the "I" and the "WE," institutional rules, disciplines, practices, and expectations are currently experienced, explicitly or intuitively, as constraints and are largely spurned in our time of attention to the "I." We don't trust them as a way to fulfill our moral polestar, which is our individual social contract.

The third reason for our current disrespect and mistrust of institutions requires a bit more background. The roots of this source of mistrust can be seen in the distinction that Robert Quinn makes between an organization's *public mission* and its *private mission*.[23] Quinn notes that an organization's *public mission* is what it announces to the world as its purpose. For example, the public mission of a school system is some version of the claim that it exists for the education and preparation of children for the future. This is what school systems tell the public that they do.

However, over time all organizations and institutions quite naturally develop an internal *private mission,* which is defined as the satisfaction of the most powerful of the constituencies connected to the organization. Using the example of a school system again, the private mission leads school boards to make decisions that will focus on satisfying their most powerful constituencies: teachers, parents, state and federal mandates, and local community groups. In time this private mission of a school can easily overshadow the interests and needs of the students, despite the fact that the students are the primary clients of the public mission. So . . . reason number 3:

3. Over time, all established institutions naturally gravitate toward their private mission of constituency satisfaction.

> This is not a nefarious choice. Rather it is the natural and constantly growing reorientation that happens over time requiring leaders to attend to the internal needs of the organization and the people who work in it. Under another name it is also known as "mission creep," in which the attention of leaders is diverted from their intended purpose.
>
> For example, well-established mature institutions like Mainline Protestant denominations continue to announce their public-mission—such as United Methodism's "we make disciples of Jesus Christ for the transformation of the world." This is an outward-focused mission statement to bring healthy and healing change to both individuals and communities as the target of Christian mission. But, beginning with the decline of membership and resources in the mid-1960s, the anxiety-fueled, private mission of institutional survival took over with attention shifting to the strongest internal constituencies: the security of clergy as a professional group, efforts of congregational development to increase the flow of resources of people and dollars to support established buildings and programs, the fulfillment of the letter-of-the-law of institutional management as outlined by books of polity. From inside the institutional organization, this attention to the constituencies of clergy, congregations, and denominational law felt like the fulfillment of fiduciary responsibility—good leadership. From outside of the institutional organization, people intuited that the church announced one thing about its purpose (its public mission) but then focused its attention inwardly on its own clergy, lay leaders, resources, and rules (its private mission). It became another reason for mistrust.

Because of these three drivers, trust has become a major topic in the current consideration of our cultural relationship with all institutions in this time of epochal transition. We need institutions in order to develop as individuals, in order to nurture ourselves and others in community, and in order to structure our national lives in equitable ways that won't harm others. This is fundamentally necessary and deeply needed. But not trusted. In this next cultural turning, trustworthy institutions will once again be essential to the individual and to the common good.

So, it is that trustworthiness may be the first and most immediate steps that our current institutional leaders must address as a short-term goal in the long-term cultural chaos of our turning. Despite the decades of recent history in which we have learned our distrust in institutions, the steps toward trustworthiness are possible. Recovering trust, however, will take the deep and quiet courage of our leaders who have become habituated to rewards from the strong constituencies within their organizations who want to be satisfied and secure. Leaders will need to realign their attention and resources to their public mission—a shift that will not be highly regarded by the internal constituencies that seek attention and resources to assuage their own anxiety.

Trust is built by both the leaders of organizations and by the organizations themselves when they are able to earn positive responses to two essential questions:

1. Does the organization actually do what it says it will do?

   This is simply the question of the public mission and the why of the institutional organization. Does the organization know its why? In many cases the leaders of our institutional organizations will need to go back to recover and restore the public mission. But to do what one says one will do is an essential act central to inviting trust from others.

2. Do the leaders have the courage and the capacity to do what they say they will do?

It is necessary first to reclaim and recommit to the public mission. But, in many cases, to take long established institutional organizations back to their public mission means to steer away from imbedded practices and the rewards given by the constituencies who shape the agenda of the private mission. Leadership is always a tenuous act because it requires and depends upon followers, but followers can always revolt or leave if not satisfied. It takes courage—quiet courage—for leaders to hold up purpose continuously and clearly in their organization and to invite others to step forward to serve purpose even when it is against their own security, satisfaction, and self-interest.[24] But this is the element of courage and capacity that is at the heart of trust. Purpose—the public mission of an institution, it's "why"—does not live on lip-service. Once courage and capacity is evident, people will once again risk their trust.

I argue that institutions are necessary and needed. We depend upon them to shape our own individual lives and to shape our communities. This truth about institutions is critically important in the present chaotic moment of our cultural turning as we oscillate between our attention to the "I" and the "WE." Without strong, trustworthy institutions, we will strain unsuccessfully to reorient ourselves away from the current over-expression of the self, individual liberties, and personal truths. It is our institutions of morality that require us and give us the means to serve something greater than ourselves.[25] Particularly in the reestablishment of the institutional system of morality where religion thrives, we provide both reason and means for individuals to "be there" for one another.[26]

Because we are still in a moment in which our culture is shaped by dominant individual values, giving attention to our institutional organizations of morality is a deeply countercultural activity. To want to reclaim and reestablish the rules and practices that serve the common good is clearly to steer into the wind, which is heavy and difficult sailing. As Heclo wrote, to think institutionally is "a kind of subversive resistance movement against the prevailing trend of things."[27] It is increasingly clear that congregations are meant to be countercultural in an "I" culture that is at a turning.

For a culture, a people who continually demonstrate having swung too far toward individual values and liberties, a countercultural push toward the common good is a necessary antidote. Hence, I continue to argue that congregations in this moment are to take seriously and openly claim their countercultural institutional identity. But a countercultural institution must clearly understand its own why—the very treasure that it holds. A countercultural movement requires a countercultural story—an alternate narrative—and it is to that different story that we now turn. It is a different story that is carried by religion and the primary institutional organization of religion—the congregation.

CHAPTER 5

Jesus Loves Me, and the Stories We Tell Ourselves

The Treasure in Our Clay Pot

A PRIMARY TASK OF INSTITUTIONS OF MORALITY IS TO CARRY THE story that will provide meaning for people's lives. The story provides an explanation of why the world is as it is. With a conviction of how the world is and how it works, a person has a clearer sense of how to be and to thrive in the world—what actions and attitudes are required, what behaviors are supportive, what relationships to form. Meaning is made when a person's behavior and relationships align in the world with purpose. Such institutional stories are best when they are clear and simple, even if in their simplicity they hold much detail.

The story that the congregation holds is its true treasure, primarily because it describes a world of love and interdependence. It counters competition and scarcity with caring relationships and sufficiency. But, after thousands of years and millions of followers, the Christian story has become quite complex and complicated with so many variations, applications, interpretations, and emphases that its power to guide and heal easily becomes diffuse. The simple form of the narrative needs to be revived and retuned to the times, particularly at the time of a turning. What is currently needed from the institutional congregation is the clear and fundamental story of the world and our place in it, from the perspective of biblical faith. We need a simple story.

In a story oft told with multiple variations. Swiss Calvinist theologian, Karl Barth, was on a lecture tour at the University of Chicago in 1962 when a student asked if he could summarize his life's work in a single sentence.[1] Now, Karl Barth was not a simple man. His groundbreaking work on the book of Romans was published in 1921. His multivolume theological summa, *Church Dogmatics*, began publication in 1932, and by his death in 1968, was still incomplete. As a theologian he was deep, complex, and prodigious. Nonetheless, he told the student questioner yes, he could provide a summary, and then offered his single sentence: "Jesus loves me, this I know, for the Bible tells me so."

It is a stroke of genius to be able to face into the confusing complexity of a topic, issue, or situation and be able to name the clear and central truth on which it all hangs. In such cases, to name a simple truth demands prolonged attention to deep and complex thought before clarity can appear. As Supreme Court Justice Oliver Wendell Holmes famously said, "For the simplicity on this side of complexity, I wouldn't give you a fig. But for the simplicity on the other side of complexity, for that I would give you anything I have."

Simplicity on the other side of complexity is essential when searching for the countercultural story on which a people, or a faith, can thrive, for ours is a complex and confusing world. Beyond the obvious complexity of technology, ours is a world also made complex by the volume of information and choices as well. Consider that there are now so many laws and rules of legal procedure that any case of law can be argued from two competing sides, each with what is thought to be compelling evidence of the rightness of their position—even in the face of an obvious wrong. Journalists continually engage in point-counterpoint arguments over the same facts. And, as noted, our hyperbolic attention to the individual easily elevates anyone's opinion or perspective to the level of truth—at least for that individual. We have arrived in a place where individuals, and their tribes, adhere to simplistic truths that *deny* the complexity beneath them. These are the empty simplicities easily captured because they deny or avoid the complexity facing them. This includes the worldviews of social justice, techno-utopianism, and atavism that can only see the individual and choose to deny the complexity and difficulty of community with its need for a common good and a public square. In a world filled with difficult complexities, it is just easier to claim empty simplicities. We have arrived in a world, not of clarifying truths, but of multiple competing simplicities that lead to gridlock. If you and I each hold to an easily simplified singular truth, and if our truths oppose each other, then we have no way of moving ahead together. We are stopped dead in the water by a nihilism and narcissism of individual claims to truths that we have allowed to go too far. Gridlock.

There must be some way to push back on the deadlocked individualism that has stopped us in our tracks. We are now trapped by simplistic positions that we believe we must accept without regard for the rich and confusing complexity that is the context surrounding us. So, Russia can invade Ukraine claiming that it is on a peace-keeping mission. So, Republicans can oppose any and everything that Democrats seek to move ahead by claiming that an election was stolen. So, Protestant denominations can internally contest and divide over a mere half-dozen biblical references to homosexuality, waging opposing opinions about God's nature and intent. So white supremacists can claim superiority by referencing a history from which others have been excluded. So political conspiracists can tell stories that release them from laws all others must follow. These are all simplicities on *this side* of complexity that can provide an easy way for any side to be right and to claim their preference over others. Such simplicities seek comfort in neat "truths" that allow no space for others. For these we should not even offer a fig.

In such a divided world beset by gridlock, there must be a way to push back in an effort to find other ways ahead. As philosopher Ken Wilber argued, "The pain and suffering that both sides feel is, I believe, the result of identifying with a much too narrow view, and a more expansive stance offers genuine release, while still allowing one to work on whatever side one wishes."[2] A more expansive stance offering genuine release from the constraints of oversimplified truths that serve only the individual and their chosen tribe. Wilber argues that humanity has "evolved" too far in its search for individual freedoms and acceptable differences, so we are now confronted with an emptiness in which there is no agreeable space in which "all" can live. William Sloan Coffin once said in a sermon at the

Riverside Church, "If you're at the edge of an abyss, the only progressive step is backwards."[3] Our cultural evolution of individual rights and freedoms has brought us to the abyss of a community-less tribal condition in which we do not speak to important things with one another unless already assured that our listeners already agree with us. There is no space that welcomes multiple thoughts or needs. To counter the absence of agreeable space we are now at a cultural moment in which the natural oscillation of counterbalancing values is seeking a way to step back and to swing again toward the common good where there is more space for all. It is time to step back and recover the common good, an understanding of community and the foundation of a covenant that determines our relationship both with God and with one another. Stepping back is the way ahead. Here we begin to glimpse the need for the institutional congregation.

THE WORK OF THE INSTITUTIONS OF MORALITY
Finding that agreeable space in which we can all live is the natural purpose and work of the institutions of the system of morality. Keep in mind that Jonathan Sacks identified the system of the institutions of morality as the primary space of cultural cooperation. The two other systems of the economy and the state are supported by institutions that are naturally competitive and divisive because they attend to the creation and distribution of wealth and power. In both of the systems of the economy and the state, by design, there is not enough to go around, and there are no built-in assumptions of equity and sharing. Conversely, it is the system of the institutions of morality that are cooperative and collaborative. And as is obvious, being cooperative and collaborative is not easily done when working from the values of the individual "I" position. It takes cultural attention to the values of "WE" to undergird the cooperation and collaboration that escapes the gridlock of opposing singular positions. It is the institutions of morality—congregations, nonprofits, social agencies, marriage, democracy—that require us to think long-term about purpose as opposed to short-term about personal gratification. These institutions ask us to attend to things greater than ourselves. As Sacks wrote, "One significant contribution of religion today is that it preserves what society as a

whole has begun to lose: that strong sense of being there for one another, of being ready to exercise mutual aid, to help people in need, to comfort the distressed and bereaved, to welcome the lonely, to share in other people's sadnesses and celebrations."[4] Diminished over recent decades by the cultural values of the individual, we need to reinvest ourselves in the institutions of morality, such as congregations in our search for the more expansive stance of the common good which is now so glaringly absent.

"The more expansive stance" that Wilber wrote of is what the institutions of morality bring to the table. It is the hard-won simple truth of congregations at their best. I have deep appreciation for the quick aside that Tom Long included in his book on Christian testimony. He described a gathered congregation as an "odd thing"—a place where there will always be other people that we would not choose to be with in any other setting.[5] Because congregations deal in hard-won, simple truths of a biblical faith that applies to and includes all people, not just tribal subsets of preagreeable people, there is always room for people different from ourselves. The expansive space is intended to include some who are different from us (even disagreeable to us), but nonetheless "belong" just as we do because of the shared stories of faith that bring us together. In the search for a shared story in which all can live, congregations, at their best, welcome all seekers and intend to include with them all the differences they bring. Anywhere else we now go in our encounters with the systems of the economy, the state, and with consumer corporations, we are invited only into tribes of agreement or prefit categories of market segments.[6] Tribes and market segments are again simplicities that deny the complexities of who we really are and who we can be.

THE STORIES WE TELL IN OUR SEARCH FOR MEANING

At the heart of the life of every individual is the search for meaning. As I have been defining meaning, it is to be found in our efforts to understand how the world is as it is, and to understand our own individual place in that world. Our search for meaning brings us to choose what story we will tell ourselves about how the world works and how we are to be in it. Whether we are constrained to a narrow gridlock or offered a more expansive space that allows and includes others depends greatly on what story we choose and how we understand ourselves as actors in that chosen story.

Some stories that we tell ourselves about how the world works are narrow and limiting. They are stories of a world short on resources and opportunities, which lead people to find their place in the story by competing against others over what they believe is scarcity. These stories explain why some people have, or deserve, more than others and what needs to be done—what alliances need to form—in order to get more. Such stories explain poverty and famine on large, even global scales. This is certainly the root of the story of atavism as told in chapter 1, but they are also stories of our own impoverishment because they are continually framed by what we see as missing. In her remarkable work on understanding money, activist and fundraiser Lynne Twist captures this story at the very individual, personal level:

> For me, and for many of us, our first waking thought of the day is "I didn't get enough sleep." The next one is "I don't have enough time." Whether true or not, that thought of not enough occurs to us automatically before we even think to question or examine it.[7]

Even for people who live in the very heart of developed nations in environments of abundance, it is possible to tell ourselves the story of scarcity; the story of how we forever have "not enough" in a world that fails to provide or allow for what we think we need. Those who choose these stories define their daily life by what is missing, what is limited. Such stories about resources, about the economy of life, are powerful and formative in the ways we approach education, work, consumption, and one another. At the base, these are stories of competition in which meaning is formed by winning—by acquiring as much as possible in order to provide personal security in a world of limited resources. These are stories supported by the institutions of the economy.

Other stories are about power and the ways in which the politics of governing control our place and potential as participants in regional, nation, and global communities. These stories assume that there are some subsets of people who have agency and control, people who can come to an agreement on how to make the world work and how the rest of us should live in it. Frequently, these are stories in competition with one another, offering narratives with different centers of control. Examples of these narratives of competition can be found in the work of Yuval Levin as he diagnoses the polarized political gridlock currently experienced by Americans.[8] He notes that Republicans essentially still look back to the era of Ronald Regan in the 1980s and the Regan Revolution of trickle-down economics. In this story, the rich and powerful are able to use their wealth and power so that the effect of their own self-interest will trickle down to benefit those who do not have wealth and power. This story is a modern iteration of the "invisible hand" economic theory introduced by Adam Smith in the eighteenth century. Comparatively, he notes that Democrats largely reflect back to the 1960s and the Great Society of Lyndon Johnson. In this competing story, there are people without wealth and power who do not have the capacity to change their circumstances and, therefore, must depend upon the government to bring resources, equity, and justice to them. These are stories supported by the institutions of the state.

These political stories of how the world is places people into the story according to the established markers of class, education, status, and membership in demographic and ethnic alliances. It is notable that both of the political narratives that Levine identifies are nostalgic. They look back into history to times that were felt to be more controllable—seeking answers to current gridlock and the lack of movement on social problems by looking back, not looking ahead. One of the central critiques of the current narratives of politics and governance is that few, if any, are forward looking with clear or compelling arguments of how to move into the next turning of our future. The confusion and complexity of our current gridlock has captured these stories in a nostalgia that leaves us without convictions of how the world can work and how individuals can thrive together in a potentially different future.

This quite naturally brings us to the narratives of the individual—the self—which have also been on the ascent. Narratives of the competitive self are clearly the root of the stories of the social justice and the techno-utopian movements. Here, we now enter the area of anti-institutional stories that seek to explain the world without the constraints and disciplines of institutions. For example, in her exploration of the self-care movement, which is a part of the techno-utopian worldview, Burton describes this narrative of self-care as a story of the division between the authentic intuitional self (both body and soul) versus the artificial, malevolent forces of society and its expectations—the contest between the needs of the self and the demands of the others.[9] This is a story that we can choose, where the "other" is a potential enemy because of the multiple ways in which others can distract and demand one's attention away from the self. In this narrative, "sinfulness is diverting one's attention from sufficient self-care and self-attention as evidenced by false modesty, undeserved humilities, and refusing to shine bright." This is a story that rests close to the center of the "moral polestar" that Heclo identified earlier in which it is assumed that the individual has the freedom, the right, even the moral responsibility to seek personal pleasure and satisfaction. In this story, the way the world is as it is focuses solely on the individual, and meaning in such a world is found by living the best life one can. Diet, exercise, the acquisition of money, and capitalistic consumption become primary tools of faithfulness in this worldview.

The stories available to us are multiple and varied. Putnam and the work of cyclical historians help us to see that the shift from "I" to "WE" is a baseline tension in human history in which we oscillate between our stories of meaning in a search for balance. There is some comfort in knowing we have been here in this balance before. However, one real difference of this present cultural oscillation is that the American people are not limited to only a few widely shared, basic stories of the world. This time, as individuals in an "I" culture, we are free to make up our own stories and to form our own tribes of people who agree with us. Consumer capitalism, with its tools of advertising and marketing, have provided us with an array of goods and services never known before—so, we believe we can have things in any way we like them. Similarly, the Internet has taught us that our very identity is malleable, fungible, and can shape-shift to accommodate whatever tribe we are dealing with in the moment—so, we can become whomever we choose to be. So, instead of being poised at this moment of a turning with only a few fundamental competing stories to explain our world, we are now in search of a new "WE" with a vast array of individual and tribal stories that will further complicate any search for the common good. Some of these stories are pernicious in their service to the self, such as the narratives of white supremacy, anti-Semitism, and the ideologies of hate. Some are wildly distorting, such as the narratives of conspiracy like Q-Anon, which posits the existence of cabals of organized political evildoers. Many are anti-institutional. All in all, a significant number of the stories that we now call upon to explain the world to ourselves are based on scarcity, fear, and the search for power. These are stories that have brought us to surges of global populism, the resurgence of racism, homophobia, and anti-immigrant nationalism. They are narratives that may strengthen and embolden some, but only as they disenfranchise and impoverish others. They are, by definition, the easier simplicities on this side of a real complexity that offer comfort and assurance to the self at the expense of the other. None of these stories wrestle with the complexity of a world in which all people belong and are valued.

So, we are now a people in search of a different story—one that captures the balance of a needed civility, an ethos of manners, an importance of community, and the connection of a shared creation. We are betwixt and between, caught at the beginning of 2021 in the uncertainty of a January 6 capital insurrection of warring tribal truths, and a January 20 inauguration, which spoke of a unified people who no longer lived in red and blue states. How we move ahead is in the balance and not yet determined. The story we choose to live by—the way we choose to understand the world and how we are to live in it—will determine the future. We are now at a place where the institutions of morality, the presently diminished third system of our lives, must offer their alternative narrative in a way that will sustain us. It is time for the church to speak again.

The Alternative Narrative of a Biblical Faith

Here is where we begin to sort through the complexity of our own inheritance as an institutional church to uncover or, perhaps, recover the treasure in our clay pot. This is our pearl of great price—the simple story that can only be found on the other side of complexity.

Recall where we are in the argument. As noted in chapter 2, congregations, as organizations within their communities, have historically played multiple roles that changed and adapted as those communities changed their character and nature over time. As noted in chapter 3, congregations enjoyed higher profiles and stronger cultural voices at times when the values of "WE" were on the rise (most recently from the 1920s into the 1960s)—and suffered diminished profiles and voices in the times of "I." In chapter 4, the distinction between the *values* of the institutional congregation and the *organization* of the institutional congregation helps to clarify the importance of *what* congregations offer as different from the *ways and means* by which they go about their work. The values of an institution are their *why* and are essential. The organization of an institution is the *how* and must be malleable, adaptable, and ultimately expendable. With all these complexities of changing historical organizational forms, with the shifting values of an oscillating culture, and with the current organizational anxiety of leaders in search of resources and programs to sustain the buildings and programs that we now hold, we are learning that the real value of our congregations is not in the programs, practices, or buildings. The treasure that we hold is our story—the steady, simple, fundamental, alternative narrative of a biblical faith that embodies the knowledge and values of the *why* that the institutional congregation holds and seeks to practice. *The biblical story that congregations hold of how the world is as it is and our place in the world is what matters.*

The present members and leaders of established congregations need to come to terms with the reality that the current ways by which the institutional congregation offers the treasure of its story has less and less appeal to the continuing generations who are shaped more and more by a capitalist economy and the omnipresent Internet that, between the two, promise everything, even that which cannot be delivered. What the institutional congregation must learn from our recent, decades-long search through church growth strategies, program proliferation, and marketing strategies is that our purpose will not be accomplished by getting more effective or more inventive with what we do, but in getting clearer—simpler—in what we know with the conviction of faith. "Jesus loves me, this

I know, for the Bible tells me so." The simplicity on the other side of complexity.

The Biblical Text as a Second Thought

The biblical text challenges our multiple dominant cultural stories by locating power not in the state, the economy, or the self, but where it has always been—in the hands of the creative One God.

> *The biblical text functions among us as a "second thought," coming after the initial description of our life in the world according to the dominant metanarrative of our society. One function of redescription is to protest against that initial description and to insist that the initial presentation of reality is not an adequate or trustworthy account. The initial description of our current context may be a secular account of reality, preoccupied with power and the self-indulgent use of power in a way of entitlement or, alternatively, it may be a supernaturalist fiedeistic presentation of reality that misconstrues the claims of faith. Either way, such a description of reality will not do, for it distorts the truth of God's hidden reality amid the ordered workings of the world.[10]*

So wrote Walter Brueggemann in *The Word That Redescribes the World*. The biblical narrative tells of an economy that is sufficient to counter our fear of scarcity and our search for abundance. It tells of a world that always provides community, space for the common good. Most important ,the text tells of a way to be with God and a way for people to be with one another.

For example, such a redescription is in the text of the story of the Exodus, one of the archetypal narratives that stand at the center of the Judeo-Christian understanding of how the world is as it is and how we fit into it. In the Exodus story of the Israelites' escape out of slavery in Egypt, the various narratives of our current world would place all their bets on Pharaoh. In terms of the economy, Pharaoh held all the riches. He owned the land, reaped a portion of all harvests, built palaces and temples in his own name. In terms of power and the state, he set the rules, enslaved who he chose, and had an army to enforce what he claimed. These are the narratives of the world that now drive our current culture— the explanations based on resources, technology, power, control, and fear.

The alternative narrative of the biblical faith offers a very different treasure. Here the power belongs to God, and resources are made available as needed. In the face of mighty Pharaoh, God calls on a slave who has trouble speaking and doesn't know which way to go to lead the people out of slavery. Escaping slavery in this biblical story doesn't require power, wealth, or even oratory. When Pharaoh commands his mighty, unequalled army to recapture the slaves, God commands the winds and waters of the Red Sea to part to win the war without battle. While Pharaoh owns the land and controls the food, God provides manna each day—not in abundance, never in scarcity, always enough. Where Pharaoh's Egypt is a scripted land with everyone in their place consigned to individual roles of imposed status and assigned schedules, God puts people in an unformed wilderness as an unformed people who are to reorder themselves as a people in community in pursuit of a covenant promise. This is an archetypal narrative. It is a story explaining how God's reality is not just different from the stories of the world, but a promise that the difference is possible and available to those willing to find their own way through the wilderness to live into the biblical story.

The biblical text tells a story that is different from others. As Brueggemann argues, the text reveals the "truth of God's hidden reality amid the ordered working of the world." Such stories—well told and well understood so that we can find ourselves in them—open the more expansive space that we are now in search of in our gridlocked experience because they are stories of a very generous creation where power, resources, and control are not just limited to those who can dominate others. These are critical stories of a more expansive space through very simple truths that are the natural treasure held within the institution of the congregation. But to serve our needs in this cultural moment, the institutional church must tell this biblical story *in its simplest form.* The story must be told from its very foundation, from the bedrock on which all else that we have learned by faith rests. Our future hope will be carried by the institutional congregation if it is able to shake free of its own internal competing interpretations and partial truths and live openly as a model of its most basic truth—its essential story.

The Alternative Simplicity of the Biblical Text: 613 to 11 to 3 to 2

Standing against the easy oversimplifications of the current cultural stories that deny the complexities of our world, the biblical narrative offers a life-giving simplicity that has withstood the many complexities of time throughout the ages. Beneath the biblical tales and the practices and traditions of faith, there is an essential simplicity that announces an intended, different, and possible world. That essential simplicity is founded on the reality that we are all, in our immense range of fractal differences and diversity, part of the same creation and the same creative force; we are responsible for one another.

That which seems complex finds its best foundation when boiled down to true simplicity. Consider how a footnote in the Common English translation of the Bible points out this movement from complexity to simplicity.[11] It notes that the full canon of Hebrew law begins with the 613 commandments attributed to Moses. The 613 commandments are the sum of both the written and the oral law of Israel.

Six hundred and thirteen commandments are complexity itself. Having that number of laws gives everyone plenty with which to work. In that great mix of rules, anyone can find one or two commandments that agree with their worldview or address their particular concern and can argue why he or she is right and others wrong. This is the competition of perceptions and convictions we now experience in the swirl of our current economic, political, self-framed, pernicious, conspiratorial, and ultimately unsatisfying stories. For example, focusing on just one, two, or six of those rules, as if they are determinative just because they are connected to an issue, such as homosexuality, can only offer division from others who choose different texts to point to. With 613 commands, we can all find something to hang our worldview on that will allow us to argue pleasantly or combatively for our own advantage, but perhaps never find purpose or community. And, arguing which of our competing commands has precedence or priority deepens the game without finding any winners. Complexity is a great game to play, but it makes it even harder to find the life-giving simplicity on the other side. It cannot lead to stories of meaning.

However, it is noted in Jewish literature that the early rabbis discussed the 613 commands and sought from them a simplicity that would give life. Beginning with the full 613 commands, the rabbis noted that David *reduced the law to 11 commands* (Psalm 15) and that Micha *reduced the law to 3* (Micha 6:8). The eleven commands of Psalm 15 do not jump easily to the lips: live free of blame; do what is right; speak truth sincerely; do no harm with your talk; do no harm to a friend; don't insult a neighbor; despise those who act wickedly; honor those who honor God; keep a promise even when it hurts; don't lend money with interest; and don't accept a bribe against any innocent person. More familiarly, the further reduction of all of the laws down to three by Micah come to many lips more easily: do justice; love mercy; and walk humbly with God.

From 613 to 11 to 3. It is not a difficult step to realize that Jesus reduced the laws one more step to two. Jesus was approached by a lawyer—insincerely by the way. The lawyer hoped to use the 613 commandments and the competing powers of Israel and Rome to trap and derail Jesus. So, the lawyer asked, "Teacher, what is the greatest commandment in the law?" The well-known adage about lawyers is that they never ask in court any question for which they don't already know the answer. This adage applied to the lawyer who confronted Jesus as well. For the lawyer was confident, knowing that with 613 commandments to choose from, with the stories of the covenant Jews and the conquering Romans swirling about in competition (i.e., with so many answers swirling about), there was no choice that Jesus could make with which he could avoid being denounced as a fraud. This was the contest between the scribes (the experts of the law), along with the Pharisees (the strictest observers of the law), against Jesus, who called out the insincerity in the ways they used the law to get along and personally thrive in a Roman-dominated world. In the face of such complexity, Jesus named the simplicity on the other side:

He replied, "You must love the Lord your God with all your heart, with all your being, and with all your mind. This is the first and greatest commandment. And the second is like it: you must love your neighbor as you love yourself.

Matthew 22:37–39

From 613 to 11 to 3 to 2.
And then Jesus concluded by saying:

All the Law and the Prophets depend on these two commands.

Matthew 22:40

Commenting on Jesus' conclusion in verse 40, biblical scholar Richard Hays noted that "these two commandments, in other words, are not merely the greatest or the most important, the ones at the top of the list; rather they have a systemic, structural, and hermeneutical role. All the other commandments in the Torah are suspended from these two pillars."[12] Simplicity on the other side of complexity. Jesus drew from the deep well of Hebrew texts that were so well-known to his listeners (from the Shema of Deuteronomy 6:4–5, and from the Levitical Holiness Code in Leviticus 19:18) to, as Hays suggests, reconfigure the Torah to a worldview, a narrative, in which love is the most determinative requirement: Love of God and love of neighbor. Honoring the one God that made us all. Knowing that serving the other is just as important and as necessary as serving ourselves.

This is the great treasure now to be found in the values of *the institutional congregation* that is housed in the earthen vessel of *the organizational congregation*. Our world does not need congregations and denominational leaders to announce which political party is right. Political parties are currently a part of the gridlock of oversimplistic tribal competitions. The world needs the congregation to tell its own essential story—the very simple biblical story of love—that our essential purpose is to love God and to love our neighbor. This is the simple story of the institutional congregation that is needed and must be reintroduced from the countercultural position of faith. In contrast to cultural stories of meaning that separate, divide, and put people against each other, there is the very different story of biblical love. The biblical story offers the expansive space that Wilber sees as so necessary to all and stops no one with explanations of exclusion. The biblical story gives meaning by saying that the world can be described without scarcity, dividing differences, and the power of politics. The biblical story that shows how the world works begins with a creative hand that rests over all—all people, all nations, all nature. This biblical narrative, in describing the world as it is, also provides a place and a way for us to be in that world. In the telling of the story in this way our place—our purpose—is to honor the God who made us all. Our place is to love and care for others as we would love and care for ourselves. This biblical narrative that explains the world and our place in it is clearly a story of "WE." The alternative story held by the currently diminished institutions of morality provides the expansive space we seek again in order to allow us to move ahead individually and together.

The Messianic Family

So, here is our first life-giving simplicity: the dual commandment. We are all made by the creative hand of God and, so, are to honor that One God—acknowledging how the power of that One God relieves us from the fear and scarcity that belong to the stories told by the world. The biblical story tells how the world is as it is (how the world can be as it can be) and then offers us our place in that world. Our place in this biblical story—the way in which we can find meaning—is to love and feel responsible for our neighbor. It is the fundamental and simple narrative of understanding that the world works best when we love God and love one another. It is the alternative to the world's stories in which fear, scarcity, competition, self, diminishing isms, or conspiratorial fantasies are the focus.

To this first simplicity comes a second necessary simplicity that addresses the question, "Who then is our neighbor?" In the current stories operative in our world, which are defined by the importance of the "self," the "neighbor"—the one to be loved and included—is the person or persons who are most like ourselves and who most agree with us. In these stories that the world tells, the neighbors are the people of our chosen tribe as measured by race, creed, nationality, wealth, political position, sexual orientation, search for wellness, conspiratorial agreement . . . indeed, the world has so many definitions of neighborliness, all of which exclude some people even as we search for community.

The second necessary simplicity of a biblical faith is also hard-won after sorting through the complexity of the many possibilities of neighbor. Jesus moved the story from 613 laws to 2. Paul then moved the story about the neighbor from the complexity of determining who are the observant, the faithful, the similar, the few—to the clarifying simplicity of the "all"—the messianic family.

Through the story of Paul, we are offered a description of a world that works because the neighbor is defined as everyone. This is not at all the assertion of any of the current world stories in their competitive variants now at hand. It is, however, the second hard-won simplicity of the institutional congregation at its best. Here we turn to a different archetypal story in the biblical text—the story of Saul's conversion on the road to Damascus. It is the story of the transformation from Saul, the law-observant Jew, to Paul, the Apostle of Jesus Christ (Acts 9:1–19).

Conversion is not always a total change of mind or behavior—not necessarily a reversal or rejection of what is already known. It can also be a completion or fulfillment of what is known, by seeing something in a new way so that the result is life altering. This is the case with Paul, as argued by New Testament scholar N. T. Wright.[13] As an observant Jew, tutored and trained in the law, Paul was a first-rate carrier of the Hebrew story of the covenant, the story of God's promise and love for the Jews. The Damascus Road experience did not change this story up to that point. Instead, it extended this story to a new conclusion because as the scales fell from Saul's eyes, he saw what he already knew, but in a new way. The covenant with Israel's God was still there from the time of the Exodus. Except now, through Jesus Christ, Saul—becoming Paul—saw that the story was not just the story of the Jews but of everyone and anyone willing to live by the new telling, which included the death and resurrection of Jesus. The neighbor to be loved was everyone and anyone. "Paul believed that, through Jesus and his death, the One God had overcome the powers that had held the world in their grip. And that meant that all humans, not just Jews, could be set free to worship the One God."[14] There were no longer to be walls of hostility dividing Jews from Greeks, men from women. Paul began to speak of his work as a ministry of reconciliation.

Wright notes that each time Paul traveled to a city he would go immediately to the synagogue to speak with the people most like himself. He would tell the Jews the story that they already knew, rehearsing the steps from Adam through Abraham, Exodus, David, exile, Isaiah, the Psalms, and the Messiah. You can imagine heads nodding with recognition and agreement as well as smiles directed at this studious and accomplished storyteller. But then Paul would surprise them with a new conclusion to the story that the people thought they already knew. He would tell how the Messiah was Jesus, crucified and raised from the dead and, therefore, how the covenant and promise, the story that they knew and held for themselves, was actually intended for everyone. Paul would offer his central argument:

> *Since the defeat of the powers had been accomplished by Jesus' death, through which sins were forgiven (the sins that kept humans enslaved to the powers in the first place), the barrier to Gentile inclusion in a new "sanctified" people had gone. "Forgiveness of sins" thus entails "Gentile inclusion," and Gentile inclusion happens precisely because of "forgiveness of sins."*[15]

This was the central new understanding that changed Paul's story, name, and life. It changed a world divided into competing groups of people such as Jews and Gentiles (whites and people of color, Republicans and Democrats, heterosexuals and LGBTQ+, Americans and immigrants, etc.) into a new sanctified people sharing in a messianic family.

It was from this point in the telling that Paul's audience would begin to shift from agreeable nods and smiles to hostilities that would include physical attacks and imprisonments for Paul. The simplest truths that can hold the whole of creation and all of its people are not easily or willingly accepted by those who cling to their own stories of fear, scarcity, competition, and fantasy. The simplest stories take courage to tell and to use as a way of living in the world. The simplest stories are very hard-won on the other side of complexity. Such is the treasured story of the institutional congregation:

The Treasure of the Institution of the Church In the Time of a Turning

1. Love God.

   I cannot control what is happening around me, but I can trust, love, and align myself with the God who created a shared creation that has its own controls.

2. Love Your Neighbor.

   If I want or hope for a worthy life for myself, I must seek to provide it to all others in order to have it for myself.

3. Include Everyone.

   I cannot live without community, but the only community that can sustain me must include all others—without judgment—or it cannot sustain me.

Such is the simple story of the institutions of morality, and this is the way in which this simple story—hard-won on the other side of complexity—is told by the institutional Christian congregation at its best. It is, quite obviously, a story that has been diminished in a culture driven by individual values. It is a story in direct competition and conflict with the stories of the institutions of the economy and the state. It is a story dismissed by the stories of self-fulfillment, the dividing stories of the -isms of race and sexual orientation, and the fantasy stories of conspiracy. And it is a story that has been diffused and distorted by Christians themselves who have been caught up in the world's insistence that there be winners and losers. Yet, it is the simple, hard-won story now needed. It is the treasure held by the institutional congregation. So, it is time for the church to speak again with its countercultural story. The culture hangs in balance, seeking to oscillate again in search for a more ample space for all.

Jesus loves me this I know, for the Bible tells me so . . .

And . . .

He's got the whole world in his hand.

CHAPTER 6

Simple Treasure and the Complexity of Discipleship

SIMPLE STORIES (FOUND ON THE OTHER SIDE OF COMPLEXITY) ARE essential—but not enough. Institutions that hold such stories have captured their *why*—but then must learn how to use them to fulfill their purpose of formation. To know the story that is to guide one's life is to find meaning. To live that story in daily practice is to find purpose. To move from knowing the story at the center of one's life, to living out that story is an act of discipleship. The story is incomplete if not enabled by discipleship.

Let's recount where we are again in this argument so that there is no confusion on how the simplicity of the institutional congregation fits into our cultural chaos. The argument in this book is that we live at a time when there are dominant cultural narratives actively competing for our allegiance. The civil religions of social justice and techno-utopianism invite us to serve the self, as opposed to the common good, as the central way to live a good life. The civil religion of atavism tempts us to choose a nostalgic, but mistaken, premodern past in which dominance was reserved for certain people. To these competing narratives outlined in chapter 1 can be added the narratives of consumerism that teach us to exchange happiness for purchased pleasures easily attainable but not long lasting. And there are yet more narratives driven by economics, marketing, and multiple subsets of tribal identities.

To that grand mix I am arguing for the reclamation and inclusion of the narrative of morality—the story that claims that there is a way, through the institutions of religion, to live a good life. This is the treasured narrative held by the church. The church's narrative says that we are all meant to live in healthy community together by honoring a creative God as the source of all living and by being a good neighbor. The narrative of religion is an ancient, well-worn, life-giving simplicity. It is the simplicity on the other side of complexity I have been arguing for.

So, I argue here, with conviction, that a moral life is a simplicity. The Judeo-Christian narrative provides a way to understand the world and one's life so that there is a viable and purposeful future for creation itself, and for the many and different people within it. This moral narrative has quite naturally been suppressed as the culture oscillated toward attention to the self. And so, it is time for the church to speak again—to tell its story again, to offer its life-giving narrative in the competition for the hearts and minds of the people.

Keep in mind that the Christian narrative, at its heart, is simple and must begin simply. It is considerably simpler than many practicing Christians now make it in their disputes over ecclesial history, doctrinal standards, or practices of polity. For example, Bishop Rueben Job, who was often seen as a uniquely spiritual and sensitive leader within the United Methodist tradition, framed the Wesleyan way of life as three simple rules, which are hard-won and well formed after centuries of Christian theology and practice. To be a disciple, Job offered, is to follow three fundamental rules:

Do No Harm.

Do Good.

Stay in Love with God.[1]

Faith begins that simply. Here again is the necessary clarification that comes from the winnowing down of any version of 613 laws into a livable, simple foundation. In his writing, Bishop Job was clear that he located the three Wesleyan rules well within Jesus' dual commandments of loving God and loving neighbor. It is this clear Christian narrative that is in deep contrast with other civil religions that lead us only to ourselves or, worse, lead us on a false search for a comforting, preferential past.

Consider the way of simplicity. Job writes: "The simple rule is 'Do No Harm.' It is not that complicated. Even a child can understand what it means, and it is applicable to everyone at every stage of life."[2] There is no struggle for power here, no competition over resources. This is not a rule enhanced by the presence, or diminished by the absence, of technology. It applies to our memories of premodern, modern, and our experience of the postmodern ages. It chooses no winners or losers. Nonetheless, it does offer guidance of how to be, and how to be with others, in the world as it is. Do no harm. As a simple understanding of the world and our place in it, this deep truth is the beginning of doing theology, and certainly the beginning of discipleship, as we will see.

BEING BORN AGAIN AND SEEING ANEW

What the dominant narratives of life ask of us is to see the world in a particular way. Some narratives ask us to see the world as a contest over power and resources. Some ask us to see the world as the self in opposition to the other. The narrative of morality (of faith, of Christ) simply asks us to see the world as creative, sustaining, and as an expression of love. Love God and love neighbor. Love mercy, seek justice, and walk humbly with God. Do no harm; do good; stay in love with God.

Faith only asks that we risk seeing things in this new light and to follow what we see by aligning our behavior with it. This is conversion or, in the language of the Church, being born again. Conversion does not necessarily ask us to stop being a bad person in order to be a good person—an overly simplistic notion of the moral self. Simplistic notions such as this are often the easiest of diversions found by those who have not wrestled with the complexities of life yet seek to "convert" others to act and think as they do. More often such simplistic "conversions" lead others unthinkingly astray rather than toward wholeness. In contrast, conversion, as addressed here, asks that we look at our own experience and see it in a different light—and by seeing differently, then by being different. Again, this was the conversion of Paul on the Damascus Road.

Paul knew the covenant heritage that, as a Jew, he shared with all other Jews. It was a world he already understood. The scales that fell from his blinded eyes did not invalidate what he knew before or who he was before. The experience of conversion was to see what he already knew *in a new way*. It completed his understanding. It extended what he knew so that the covenant that was given to the Jews was simply extended to all—all, meaning Gentiles included. Seeing life in such a different way, Paul simply acted on it.

Being "born again" (John 3:3) is not a repudiation of an old life, or becoming a different person—it is seeing one's present life in a very new way, according to a new and different narrative, which requires seeing through the fresh eyes of a child. As Jesus taught, "I assure you that if you don't turn your lives around and become like this little child, you will definitely not enter the kingdom of heaven." (Matthew 18:3) What the narratives of the institutions of morality ask of us is not to be other than who we are but rather to see our life in a new and different way—along with the principles, practices, and values that will support us in shifting our behavior and relationships to be in better alignment with the new hope that we see there.

We need an example here of one who looks at what everyone else looks at but sees it in a different way because of commitment to the Christian narrative, which uncovers what is hidden. An example of one who was converted by faith. Consider Father Greg Boyle, the founder of Homeboys Industries, the largest gang intervention, rehabilitation, and reentry program in the world.[3] A Jesuit priest in Los Angeles, Father Boyle lives, works, and is friends with a host of people that the world easily calls bad, criminal, or less than human. He lives with these people in one of the poorest of urban areas deeply mired in crime, poverty, gang warfare, and drugs. Father Boyle, however, sees these same people through the guiding narrative of Jesus Christ. Through this different way of seeing, he finds only people whose circumstances have not allowed them to be healthy or whole. Father Boyle regularly and continuously explains that no healthy person chooses to be a white supremacist and thinks that white people are better than other races. No healthy person fills his or her body with drugs or alcohol so that they can't feel their own feelings and care for themselves. No healthy person turns to violence and murder to protect themselves or to get what they want. In his worldview, shaped by the institutions of morality, Father Boyle doesn't see criminals and broken people beyond salvage. He sees people who aren't healthy and whole as God intended. So, he behaves according to what he sees. In each encounter, Boyle describes what he does as give a "dose" to counter the unhealth. He gives a dose of respect by actually listening to what they say. He gives a dose of recognition by actually seeing them and knowing their names. He gives a dose of hope by offering ways for them to educate, employ, and house themselves adequately. Father Boyle will be the first to explain that his doses don't help everyone he meets, but he lives with the conviction that if they come back for enough doses, these other people will begin to see what he sees and conversion, along with health, will begin to happen to some. The narrative of faith offers a way to see the world in which there is hope—and then invites the faithful into a way of living that aligns daily behavior with that hope.

The narratives of the institutions of morality carry the stories of our faith traditions, the values of authentic relationship, and the community practices of inclusion. The usufruct of the institution of the church and the story that it carries make people like Father Boyle not just possible, but essential. Far from the way in which other dominant cultural narratives want to dismiss this story of love as simplistic or pollyannish, it is rather the deep, essential, and simple truth of how we can live together under the shared hand of God. It is the "other" story—the alternative narrative. It is countercultural, and it is carried forward by the voice of the institutions of morality such as congregations.

What we see is what we do. A culture at a turning needs the conversion that the church can offer if it is to see a new way forward. The church then needs to help people not only see the world in a new way, but to live in that world in a new way as well.

DISCIPLESHIP—THE RETURN TO COMPLEXITY AFTER THE SIMPLE IS FOUND

The simple, powerful, life-giving narrative of faith can never thrive if the simple is allowed to become simplistic. If simple is the hard-won-other-side of confusing complexity, then once found the simple must be mined deeply for the full depth of truth that it holds. That depth must then be translated into behavior in daily living. *It is the movement from seeing new to being new.* This continual shaping of behavior as an expression of a simple, true narrative is called discipleship. And discipleship is actually quite complex.

Discipleship, like the word *disciple*, is built on the old Middle English, Old French, and Latin language notions of learning and instruction. It means to train oneself (to submit oneself to instruction) in a code of behavior that meets with the standard by which one seeks to live. As soon as we move from the hard-won simple narrative by which we understand the world to the disciplined daily behaviors with which we embody that narrative, we have now crossed back from simplicity into the complexity of living. "Jesus loves me" is an unalterable, simple, life-giving truth framed beautifully by Karl Barth as the sum of his life's work. However, to be a disciple of that Jesus is our own life's work, which is quite complex. Moving the transcendent to the immanent (from Jesus' unmeasured love for all to my expression of that love for the people I share life with) goes well beyond the simplistic. It moves from guiding narrative to daily reality. Years ago, the Buddhist/Episcopal priest, Alan Watts, suggested that a good parent is to tell his or her child all about Santa Claus, only if willing to later tell the child that there is no such thing as Santa Claus. If given only the story of Santa, the child would certainly be left with a feeling of magic. But to then live beyond the overly simplistic, magical Santa story, the child must leave magic behind in order to make space for a life's instruction in the holy, mystery, awe, family, generosity, and community, which are also parts of the Christmas story. Similarly, to move from the Sunday school Jesus of childhood (a simplistic Jesus who will ultimately disappoint) to the disciplined following of the Christ (who will always constantly challenge and shape us) is a necessary step of personal and spiritual maturity. False simplistic notions provide the fantasy that the world should magically accommodate one's wishes and preferences. But, to choose a bold, simple narrative of hard-won truth and then lean into it, is to move past fantasy and to move into discipleship—a life shaped into specific and particular behaviors that reflect and make real the simple truth of the Gospel, which is the pearl of great price.

The Deep Dive of Living What One Believes (From Principle to Practice)

Let the reader beware. We are about to enter a theological discussion that is off-putting to the world, but important to the disciple. The appropriate use of this information will be considered in the last chapter.

***

At the lived level, a life of intentional faith is a complex project. It is a life shaped and supported by the usufruct of the institutional congregation. For example, to follow the simple Christian moral narrative means, among a host of things, that I am to practice generosity. It's a rather straightforward extension of recognizing the sufficiency of life I have been given by the hand of God (love of God), matched with my need to be a good neighbor to assure that others share in that sufficiency with me (love of neighbor). And it is at that point when I seek to actually practice simple generosity that I am led to the complexity of further life-giving questions and decisions. Is my generosity to reflect only my money and how I use it? Does it include my time, my attention, my spirit? Am I to be generous in these things as well—and how must my behavior reflect such generosity? What is the measure of generosity compared to what I need or seek for myself? How am I to be generous to people who hoard their own resources, time, and self? What does generosity mean to me in a developed nation set in a world of deeply undeveloped areas? For that matter, what does generosity require when I am walking a city street and approach a beggar on the sidewalk? And, if I am recognized or rewarded for being generous, is this actually generosity or selfishness?

The questions that accompany the choice of a life narrative and the subsequent steps of discipleship to live into that narrative prove curiously complex, making faith a life project of discovery with constantly changing and maturing actions. The ancient rabbis, in their constant inquiry into the meaning of the law, offer age-old examples of this rich complexity of discipleship. When considering the prohibition against stealing in the Eighth Commandment, they concluded that the commandment alluded to many forms of behavior related to theft. "Thus, failure to respond to a greeting is a theft of a fellow man's self-respect, and to win someone's gratitude or regard through deceit is a form of thievery."[4] Such self-inspection is not self-centered introspection or navel gazing, nor is it trivial, given that a person's maturity of understanding and practice depends on it. Simple truths do not lead to simplistic living. Well-founded simple truths move us from the shared universal understanding of the way the world is as it is to the finely understood particulars of our own daily decision-making. The move from the universal to the particular is always difficult and demands disciplines to keep us from either naïve or egregious missteps. The move from the universal to the particular is discipleship.

Theology that Shifts from Simple to Complex: Grace

The necessary shift from simple truths to the complexity of living rests on the foundation of the discipline of theology. Consider my own United Methodist institutional heritage of the Christian worldview as shaped by John and Charles Wesley, which holds a central focus on grace—the free and unmerited favor of God. The Wesleys described a three-tiered construction of grace reflecting the necessary shift from the simple back to the complex, from the universal to the specific. To frame the theological shift from the universal to the particular John Wesley looked at grace as having three forms: prevenient, justified, and sanctified.

"Prevenient grace is the love of God at work in our lives from the very beginning," wrote Wesley scholar, Scott Jones.[5] "Prevenient" is a form of words such as "prevent," which carries the meaning to "come before." In other words, God's prevenient grace comes before we even know it, before we can even respond to it. It has already been given even before we know it. It is universal and available to all. It exists as a simple truth that God's love falls on all, free and unmerited, no matter what differences we might find among people. One does not need to be born into any particular geography, community, or family; one does not need to be of a particular race, ethnicity, or sexual orientation; one does not need to have particular gifts, skills, or wealth to be beloved of God. God's grace is simply available to all, without restriction. As Bishop Ken Carter points out, prevenient grace finds us all "equal at the foot of the cross"—a sense of universal simplicity. It is prevenient grace that opens the door for Christians to be invitational (evangelistic)—freely inviting all others to know Christ and Christ's ways and to join in community with others to whom God's grace has also already been provided.

The second form of grace, justifying grace, is understood as not ours by the work of our own hands.[6] One does not earn it. As one becomes aware of God's grace, justification tells us that it is ours by God's own forgiveness and not by what we ourselves have done or how we might have changed. Jones notes that the Wesleys believed that the individual neither does anything to deserve such grace, nor does such grace change them, as such. Justifying grace only asks us to receive God's love as a gift that is given to all—to become aware of and receptive to it. It comes to us as we willingly live under the simple truth of God. Here again, this is a universal experience not dependent on us or our actions, and as such, all people are once again equal at the foot of the cross—the sense of universal simplicity that comes from a shared humanity in relationship with a shared God. These are key simplicities that invite, indeed ask, us to see the world in a way that includes every person as having great worth—just as we ourselves do. We cannot make it so; it just is.

Sanctification, the third of the forms of grace, however, changes the individual and moves us from the universal to the particular, from the simple to the complex. "It is logically distinguished from justification in that it is a real change God works in persons," writes Jones.[7] Methodists speak of "growing in grace toward perfection" at this stage of relationship with God—that is, we are to pattern our thoughts and behaviors more and more toward that aspirational model, which we find in Jesus Christ. Here, there is no equality of all people at the foot of the cross. We must all find and follow our own individual, particular path of discipleship. Each person, given their unique self, must grow in grace (follow and collaborate with the Holy Spirit to shape themselves in discipleship, move closer toward "perfection") by accounting their own attitudes and behaviors as necessary in order to reflect their understanding of how the world is as it is under the creative hand of God. If then all people are of great worth and equal to one another, the sanctifying grace of God is felt and lived as each individual shapes his or her own particular behavior to reflect this truth with the people he or she meets on their own daily path. Sanctifying grace is the beginning of each person's collaboration with God to address his or her own individual formation. It is aligning daily behavior with the way one sees the world through the Christian narrative of truth.

This is the Wesleyan practice of discipleship exhibiting its own clear, simple roots that give guidance. Such discipleship is guided and nurtured by fundamental institutional practices that introduce usufruct in our minds, hearts, and behavior. Indeed, it is at this point that we have our greatest need of the institution of the church. For it is in the institution that we find the values *and behaviors* that we can mirror and make our own.

Theology that Shifts from Simple to Complex: Context

If theologically the notion of grace leads the individual to their own unique and individual path of discipleship, so does the time and place in which the individual lives. The foundations of what we come to understand, to believe, require context in order to be lived. Each person's path of discipleship depends upon not only who they are but also where and when they are. Let's continue this pursuit of understanding the movement from conversion, which is seeing anew, to a life of discipleship, again along another United Methodist theological path. *Foundation* (the understanding and acceptance of God's grace freely given) must be followed by *context* (the real time and place in which the individual is to live out what they newly see). This connection of foundation and context, like the movement from the universal to the individual, is fundamental to discipleship. The hard-won simple truth of God's creative hand and our need to care for all others is the foundation won by finally observing the frailties of the temporal powers of the world and the emptiness of the overfocus on our self, along with the rebirth of seeing the connection that exists between our self and all others. This foundation then must be followed by our own specific and immediate context if we are to live out our conviction to this truth. Context supplies the specific reality in which we will address our most basic truths. Foundation is meant to be completed by context. I argue here that the context that must drive us at the time of a cultural turning requires individuals and communities to lean into convictions and behaviors of the common good.

The way in which United Methodist theology expresses the need for both foundation and context is found in the description of the theological task of the church as being both *critical* and *constructive*.[8] To do theology is to be *critical* in the sense of testing any expression of our lives against the roots and foundations from which it came. It is to be *constructive* in that it must allow for, indeed provide for, ways in which each new people can "appropriate creatively the wisdom of the past and seek God in their midst in order to think afresh about God." One's understanding and accepting of the Christian religious narrative asks the person to be *both* critical and constructive. One is to be *eternal* in order to reflect one's place in a creation that begins before time and endures with no end. But one must also be *specific* to the present moment in order to live wisely and well in that creation that is under great stress. One must be *global* since creation is shared with a vast, wide, and diverse humanity. But one must also be local in the sense defined by Tisdale, meaning "crafted for a very particular people in a particular time and place."[9] Our theology, our understanding of the world as it is, our talk about God, must be *anchored and constant* while also being *vibrant and malleable*.

Tensions that Give Life

Simplistic lives experience little tension. "Simplistic" is the simplicity that lives on the near side of complexity without doing the hard work of understanding. Simplistic living presents few challenges to those who are simplistic and offers little space to others who are different. It is like the sign in the curio shop that is meant to be amusing: "There are two kinds of people in the world—those who love bacon, and those who are wrong." The simplistic life holds no tension because others are "like me" or they are wrong.

The simple (not simplistic) life lived by the Christian narrative is quite different. It is full of tensions. The simple life acknowledges that universally all are the same by the creative hand of God—but that each must find his or her own individual path to live out God's universal grace. All are grounded in a critical and shared foundation of faith—but each must find their own constructive expression of that foundation. It is a life lived in tension.

This is no easy task for one choosing the Christian religious worldview. Such tensions and contradictions are not a satisfying condition for any people who insist upon certainty and who want agreement—especially if they want agreement from others whose particular place, moment, or experience is different from their own. This tension is at the heart of the present division between the United Methodist Church and the newly forming Global Methodist Church. Some want to live closer to constructive freshness, adapting their behavior to address changes in the contemporary culture, while others seek to hue more carefully toward critical certainty by anchoring their faith to historic creeds. This may also be, in part, some of the reason that organizational congregations, peopled by many folks who are uncomfortable with tensions and contradictions in life, are so easily captured by politics, technology, or their own constructed confessional statements of what must be believed using what specific language as litmus tests setting boundaries of who is in and who is out. The search for certainty, the critical nature of faith, if held too tightly can be a stumbling block to fully living in community because it hews too strictly to the formulation and experience that comes from an earlier time under different circumstances from our own. To have only a "critical" faith is to limit ourselves to the past without acknowledging what we now know of our own lives and our own world. Similarly, a faith that finds its expression only as constructive as it copes with increasing information, diversity of experience among an ever-increasingly diverse people, and with history that is always in the mode of including new perspectives of different people, can leave us too open with too little formation. A faith that is only critical is too rooted in its attachments to historic creeds to find meaningful application to the reality of contemporary life. A faith that is freed to explore contemporary complexity without attachment to its roots leads to experimentation without purpose. Faith becomes a lifegiving way of living only when the rooted anchor of the critical is held together with the free expression of the constructive. One foot must remain firmly planted on the foundational rock while the other foot dances freely about in exploration.

It is by these tensions (simple foundations and principles in tension with complex human behavior; the universal sameness of all people in tension with the individual differences in each person; the whole of creation in tension with the needs and wants of the self) that the worldview of the institutions of morality offer a life worth living. Instead of constraining or confusing life, such tensions make life livable. In a beautifully poetic way, David James Duncan offers a metaphor about tensions that are life giving. Duncan wrote the forward to the newly published book written by his recently deceased friend Brian Doyle in which he recalled old conversations between the two. In part he wrote,

> *we marveled that the bodies of trees are built by their downward hunger for earth and water and by their upward yearning for light. How wonderful, we agreed, that these paradoxical aims, instead of tearing a tree in two and causing it to die of indecision, cause it to grow tall and strong.*[10]

By their nature tensions do not unnerve or dismantle us. They give us a life worth living as we find our place within the tension of their opposing energies. Here then, in the religious worldview is the necessary antidote to the singular selfishness of the three godless civil religions that ask us to pursue only our own self-interests. Life is meant to be lived in the tension between one's own self-interest and the equal truth of the needs of others. Here is the corrective to Burton's "bespoke religions," which put the self in the center of a universe in which all things and all others are to orbit. Here is the tension that anchors us to the eternal while energizing us for the immediate.

THE TENSION OF I AND WE

In chapter 3, I offered a description of our current cultural moment as a "turning," one of the periodic and repeating oscillations when we as a people seek to rebalance our lives by leaning into our less dominant values. Having been too long in a time focused on the self—the "I" culture—we are yearning to lean toward the common good—the "WE" culture. This oscillating pull between the "I" and the "WE" is a fundamental tension in life. There are times in which we appropriately attend to the "I," times to attend to the "WE," and moments of turning in which we must choose in which direction to now lean. I strongly argue that in our current moment of turning the church needs to be both clear and intentional that what it has to say is in service to the common good, to the messianic community—the "WE." And the church must believe that what it has to say is important, that it has a word that is needed. The church must now intentionally lean toward the "WE." The institutional church, and the people of the church, must take the foundation of what they know and see, and in an act of discipleship offer what they know of grace and the messianic community to this particular cultural context that is lost in a-nomos.

Tensions and Polarities

This is a matter of understanding polarities. Barry Johnson defines a polarity as a set of opposites, which are interdependent.[11] Each of the poles appears to be a truth unto itself, but you cannot choose one as a solution and neglect the other because they are interdependently connected. Breathing is an excellent example. It is true that one needs to breath *in* so that the body obtains oxygen without which it cannot live. But one cannot only breath in. It is equally true that one needs to breath *out* so that the body can rid itself of carbon dioxide with which, in overabundance, the body cannot live. As Johnson points out, this is the paradoxical relationship of a polarity. "Though inhaling and exhaling are opposites, they are part of the same whole. One cannot exist without the other. In order to gain and maintain the benefits of one pole, you must also pursue the benefits of the other."[12]

"Tight" and "loose" are a similar polarity of interdependent truths. For example, it can be said that a vital organization must be clearly organized with tight and structured lines of communication and decision-making. And that is true. In contrast, it can also be said that a vital organization must be nimble and agile where communication and decision-making is loosely pushed toward those workers closest to the operational level so that they can be responsive to quickly changing situations. That also is true. Vital organizations, therefore, must be tight (true), and they must be loose (also true). They just can't be both tight and loose at the same time. Vital organizations must learn when to be tight and when to be loose- when to breathe in and when to breathe out. Tight and loose is a polarity—a necessary and life-giving tension between two essential truths that can't be practiced at the same time. Johnson's work is exceptionally helpful in showing that polarities are not problems to be solved by picking which truth/pole is right as if the other is wrong. Polarities are necessary and counterbalancing equal truths that need to be managed, not solved. In a polarity the people do not choose but rather they lean. Given that both poles are true, people must be intentional about which of the poles to lean into (to give attention to) at a particular moment, given particular circumstances.

A living, vital theology also holds such polarities. As noted, to be vital our theology, our understanding of God and our world, must be *critical*—tightly anchored to foundational, historic truths. But it also must be *constructive*—held loosely enough to translate into and make sense of a quickly changing world. Given these two equal truths, I argue with conviction that the church's alternative narrative must now be constructive—loosely held and interpreted in ways understandable to a world beset by their confusion over individualism, tribalism, and community. Steering too tightly toward required, historic, creedal understandings of faith or toward mandatory confessional statements and practices would, at this moment, leave the church incomprehensible to a world enamored by bespoke spiritual practices chosen only by personal preference.

In its fullest form, the Christian faith offers truth to individuals (personal salvation) and also to communities (social salvation). This is a polarity that mirrors the "I-WE" oscillating values of the culture, which in itself is a cultural polarity. Indeed, the mission statement of my own United Methodist denomination is to "make disciples of Jesus Christ (i.e., changed individuals) for the transformation of the world" (i.e., changed communities). What is held in common at both ends of this polarity is our deep conviction that seeing through the lens of Gospel truth (the alternative narrative) both the individual and the community will be changed in healthy and holy ways. Such change is intended. It is purposeful. Being a person of faith never intends that we be left comfortably "sitting in the pews we always sit in, singing the hymns we always sing," as my friend Tom Locke would say. To choose the alternative narrative of faith is to become intentionally changed.

But I continue with my argument. At this time of a cultural turning, what the church has that is most needing to be heard has to do with the large cultural questions of how we are to live together. Having for a time inhaled deeply in the search for personal salvation, it is now time to exhale to seek the missing social salvation of being community. If the church is to be helpful at this critical moment, it must lean into its alternative narrative of what it means to be a good neighbor and how people are intended to be part of a messianic, as opposed to a tribal, community. The Gospel narrative has the power to change individual lives to be sure, but our world, entering this particular turning of values, needs the alternative narrative of the church to show people how to live together with one another across deeply dividing differences. The church at its best is people who seek to be good neighbors and who know what a messianic community can be. The church is alternative to what the world is currently paying attention to. But the truth held by the church is important and needed now in a particular way. We have this treasure in clay pots. Our treasure is an alternative narrative of a way of life that honors the One Creative God at the center of all living, that understands the power and importance of being a good neighbor, and that welcomes without judgment all others into a shared community.

To share its countercultural treasure, the church must now exercise its gifts of *conversion*, of *discipleship*, and of *being community*—all of which it must now bend into forms recognizable to a world that has lost its ability to understand the church's language, traditions, and importance.

The Power to Convert

Using the historic language of the church, this is the time for the church to seek to convert others. I use the word "convert" in the same sense as used earlier in this chapter. It is not a conversion to a creedal belief system but a conversion of vision and understanding. It is the scales falling from Paul's eyes at the moment in which he took all that he already knew and, seeing it in a new light, extended it in a new way of life and hope because of what he saw in Jesus Christ. The church converts by inviting others, encouraging others, to see themselves and their world through the alternative lens of the Gospel narrative. It is an invitation for people to take what they already know in their lives and see it in a new light—not through the lens of the self and all of the self's attendant freedoms and liberties, but through the lens of community and the possibility of inclusion and equity. To speak biblically, it is not the contesting tribalism of the Pharisees and Sadducees but the completeness of a community that welcomes and includes the Syrophoenician woman, the leper, and the tax collector as well. It is not winners and losers, but the richness of a full community where there is no rich or poor, no people of color or white people, no straight or gay, no Republicans or Democrats—only brothers and sisters.

As Burton compellingly described, the current competing cultural narratives are fueled by fear, inadequacy, and scarcity. Political differences are parlayed into violence as people are encouraged to fight in order to claim what they have come to believe is being taken from them. Our fear of imperfect bodies and our physical disappointment with ourselves is being driven by marketing and self-care industries, not toward health but in a search to overcome anxiety and the risk of not fitting in. Assumptions of there not being enough drives an ever-expanding wedge between the haves and have-nots in a contest unfairly weighted toward the educated and privileged.

Fear, inadequacy, and scarcity are lessons learned by looking at life experiences in the particular ways our culture now offers. The Gospel alternative narrative converts people to a different view, a different perspective on life, a new way of seeing. It is not a life beset by fear and scarcity, but framed by love and sufficiency. In this new way of seeing, political differences can be converted to (re-seen as) competing strategies in search of what people need in common. Body imperfections can be converted to (re-seen as) the gifts of species diversity and richness that they are in which health becomes the goal rather than anxiety reduction and fitting in. Scarcity can be converted to (re-seen as) adequacy once it is freed from the debilitating assumptions of greed, insecurity, and privilege that currently prompts hoarding. The world deeply needs to see its own fear, inadequacy, and scarcity in a different way. The biblical alternative narrative has both the convictions and the stories to convert people to seeing what is right before their eyes.

The Power of Discipleship

If the church is to speak, if preachers are to preach, it is not just about an alternative narrative that brings a new way to look at the world as it is and how we fit into it. It is also about the behaviors, practices, and disciplines of living that allow us to fit into that new narrative. This is the critical usufruct of the institutional church. The church needs to stop its judgment about who is right and who is wrong in the contests over politics and media in order to begin the more important conversation about how to *be*, and how to be with one another. The gift that the church holds, that needs to be shared, is the disciplines that can be followed to align behavior with belief. To have "the mind of Christ within you," to "move on to perfection," to "become as a child" are expressions of the church instructing followers to bend their thoughts and actions to align with the truth that is to be found in the Christian narrative. "Adopt the attitude that was in Christ Jesus," was Paul's admonition to the Philippians (Philippians 2:5). See what Jesus saw so that you can move closer to being and doing what Jesus was and did.

Disciples need disciplines. And the disciplines must be specific (i.e., more than aspirational). They must be behavioral. In the Gospel of Luke, chapter 14 is a real countercultural story in which Jesus teaches about the topsy-turvy, upending nature of God's economy. He is at the home of one of the leaders of the Pharisees as an invited guest. In the Jewish community, the Pharisees were natural "winners"—the privileged recognizable leaders who would expect to be invited to all the right tables, in all the right homes, and seated at the places of honor. It is there that Jesus offers the alternative narrative of the messianic community. "All who lift themselves up will be brought low, and those who make themselves low will be lifted up." (vs. 11) "You will be blessed if you invite those who can't repay you. Instead, you will be repaid when the just are resurrected." (vs. 14)

In our present world where status, economy, power, and race determine who is invited to the table and who gets to sit at the preferred places, people need to hear that there is an alternative narrative, a different way to see the world, a more equitable way to live with others rather than as winners and losers. Jesus is teaching of a world so very different from the competitive worlds of scarcity presented by the institutions of the state and of the economy—so very different, but nonetheless possible.

But hearing and seeing is not enough. Disciples need disciplines. And the preacher—the congregation, the institutions of morality—need to clearly break down the wisdom of the alternative narrative into disciplines and behaviors, for our world is at this moment committed to a competition of winners and losers over who sits at the head of the table and who is to be pushed to the lowest places. Invitations get made, inclusion is offered, according to those with whom people already agree. What "truth" one ascribes to—from the radical right, the radical left, or the center—determines one's value in the eyes of others and determines what invitations of inclusion one will receive. It is a world that has lost its civility, a nation at risk of losing its democracy. So, the treasure of the alternative narrative of the congregation must be used to shape the behavior of those who would be disciples. The countercultural congregation is needed to challenge people about who they invite—to their tables, of course—but also who is to be invited into their conversations, their friendship, their personal regard, their thoughtfulness, their prayer list. This is discipleship at the level of behavior. The voice of the institutions of morality is needed to say to people that their invitations must go beyond the circle of those others with whom they already agree. They must also weave connections with those who will not naturally reciprocate their regard and thoughtfulness. This is the teaching of Matthew 14 at the behavioral level. They must invite in, and listen to, those others who are fearful in a world that has told them that something is being taken away from them. They must make room for those who have been convinced that the world is built on scarcity. They are not to invite these others while armed with arguments and weapons of their own intent on attacking faulty, competitive narratives in another contest over winners and losers, but the teachings of the alternative narrative of the biblical text simply point to the simple acts of hospitality. Invite, include, listen, show regard, be concerned, and offer rest and refreshment. As Timothy Snyder notes in his little book on the twenty lessons about tyranny from the twentieth century, the future hangs on the ability to make eye contact and small talk.[13] It is daily behavior, common curtesy, the ability to recognize and listen to others that creates an environment that invites people away from combativeness and toward a messianic community. The alternative narrative does not seek to win but to include.

People need disciplines, simple disciplines, to enable them to be with one another and they need to be as clear and specific as eye contact, small talk, invitations, and inclusion. Explicit disciplines of community are needed at times when people have overexpressed and overbelieved the importance of their own desires and in the process have abandoned the boundaries of civility. How else does one counter incidents of road rage where a passenger of one car shoots and kills the driver of the car in front of him at a stop light for having driven too slowly up to the intersection (an incident that happened recently in my neighborhood, but replicated in many others)? Behaviors that align with the alternative narrative of the biblical perspective need to be taught in all their exacting explicitness. In what specific and behavioral ways other than a gun must people learn to cope with the natural frustration that comes from living with other people? This is a holy word worthy of the pulpit. Not the narrative alone, but the behaviors that fit the narrative as well. The people of Israel had to relearn the behaviors of living with one another in order to get through their wilderness. Hence, the Ten Commandments, the ten critical ways of being with God and being with one another. When Paul wrote the memorable thirteenth chapter of 1 Corinthians, it was not intended as a poetic ode to marriage, as it is so often used in wedding ceremonies. It was behavioral instruction that Paul was giving to the Corinthian people because what he was describing as love was not what he was seeing in their behavior. When he said that love is patient, kind, and was not jealous, bragging, or arrogant, Paul was offering disciplines to be practiced, behaviors to follow, that would bring about a love that was missing.

The institutional usufruct of the church is a necessary and needed voice bearing disciplines that will make a difference at the time of a turning. The church's discipline of covenant relationships invites and sustains people in marriage relationships especially when disappointed or dissatisfied "selfs" would rather choose individual liberty over the hard work of staying in relationship. The church's discipline of forgiveness does not invite a person to fix or seek justice for something wrong that happened in the past so that it conforms to the way the person wants their past to be. Instead, the church's discipline of forgiveness shows the person behaviors to claim a future for a relationship that was bruised or damaged in the past. The disciplines of hospitality of the church do not allow people to be comfortably themselves by limiting their contact with others who are different, but they challenge growth and understanding by acts of invitation, inclusion, and listening. A culture seeking to lean into its need for "WE" needs to hear that there are ways to be community in large nontribal ways. The church is at a moment in which the culture needs to hear a voice saying clearly that there are ideas, behaviors, disciplines, and practices that can be chosen to make it possible for "WE" to once again be.

The Example of Community

It is within the power of the congregation to offer a living example of healthy community. This will be the most difficult of the challenges that the organizational congregation will face in seeking to claim its voice in the current culture in a trustworthy way. Martin Luther King Jr. famously said that the most segregated hour of the week was the time on Sunday morning when churches worship because Americans went off to worship separately as blacks, whites, and Latinos. As noted in chapter 2, as early as the late eighteenth century, "The Devotional Congregation" found ways to segment the religious marketplace according to socioeconomic strata so that communities of "equals" or "likes" could gather comfortably in worship. Congregations continue to do so today. Congregations are as much a product of their surroundings as they are an agent of values to their surroundings. Today, naively weaving politics and faith, many congregations fall prey to political parties, issues, or ideologies, as if aligning with a political position could reflect a religious conviction. Such naivete is particularly tempting at a time when the hard work of moral institutions is so easily outsourced to the eager institutions of the economy and of the state.

All of this is true, and more, making it difficult for the church to speak convincingly about community—not because of what the church knows, but because of how the church has so publicly behaved. The American congregation has been in many ways a poor example. It has been historically and contemporarily inept at managing the gross differences among people as determined by race, age, wealth, or politics. But, nonetheless, congregations do know something about community.

For the most part, congregations have always been better able to include and manage the lesser differences among people that are not telegraphed by the gross differences of age, race, or social status. The congregation still has a sense for, and an ability to deal with an "impure" market—the gathering together of people along with their differences of appearance, temperament, lifestyles, and opinions.

Such impure markets are hard to find. Noting the power that came about with the merging of technology and marketing, Joseph Turrow, in his early study of advertisers and the newly developing media world explains how the marketplace increasingly realized it had the capacity to group all people together (an "impure" market) or to segment and separate the larger marketplace into smaller slices of uniform subgroups of similar people (a series of "pure" markets.) The impure market, of course, is much larger. But pure markets of similar subsets of people are far and away easier to talk to and to sell to, thus determining the marketplace's and media's choice. This has been both a technological and commercial development with deep cultural impact. Turrow's thesis is that in the last century America experienced a major shift in that balance between society-making media (impure markets) and segment-making media (pure markets.) It is important to understand the polarity of tensions involved in sorting out society and the consequences we now live with. Writes Turrow,

> *For those who hope for a caring society, each level of medium has had its problems. Segment-making media have sometimes offered their audiences narrow, prejudiced views of other social segments.*

Similarly, society-making media have marginalized certain groups, perpetuated stereotypes of many others, and generally presented a portrayal of the world that is more the ideal vision of the corporate establishment sponsoring them than a reflection of competing visions of various publics. Nevertheless, the existence of both forms of media has meant that the potential has existed for an equilibrium between healthy social segments and a healthy collective. In the ideal scenario segment-making media strengthen the identities of interest groups, while society-making media allow those groups to move out of their parochial scenes to talk with, argue against, and entertain one another. The result is a rich and diverse sense of overarching connectedness: what a vibrant society is about.[14]

Turrow goes on to convincingly argue that America continually lost the potential to achieve the balance necessary for the connectedness of a vibrant society because of the choices made to favor the commercial and political advantages of segment-making media and pure markets. The institutions of the economy and of the state have simply, and quite naturally, followed their own competitive values to maximize their own self-interest in the culture by quickly developing new tools of communication and marketing to subdivide the people into marketing segments easily monetized. During this time of the marketing subdivision of the people, the institutions of morality deferred, perhaps unsure of the value of their own voice.

Yet, in a world that became increasingly segmented and separated into an ever-expanding array of small-segment pure markets, the congregation remains as a unique organizational institution of morality that still has some sensitivity and is still somewhat adept in the impure marketplace of the "whole" people. Yes, congregations are subject to the gross differences of race, age, wealth, and politics—to its embarrassment given its precious alternative narrative, but congregations still know how to draw individuals together across the smaller, nongross differences of personalities and peculiarities and unite them on the basis of shared faith—a belief in a shared narrative.

Congregations and denominations are not, by any means, messianic communities. Yet, they have the vocabulary for one. They have the values for one. They have the aspirations for one. At their best, they have the heart for one. They are deeply countercultural in this way at a time when the countercultural voice needs to be heard the loudest. This is one of the places where the church does not have the luxury of addressing its own sinfulness, complicity, and limitations before it speaks. It must begin to speak, publicly, about what it knows about community—even while needing to learn how to reshape its own practices of community.

The church has something life giving to say. Now the congregation has to figure out how to say it and who it is talking to.

CHAPTER 7

Where Does "WE" Live?

Finding the New Public Space and Common Good

IF, AS I ARGUE, IT IS NOW TIME FOR THE CHURCH TO SPEAK AND TO LEAN into the importance of the community and the common good—the "WE"—then it is important to ask, "Where is the 'WE' that is to be spoken to. Where does 'WE' now live?"

Earlier I wrote of the 1950s as the height of our most recent oscillation of cultural cohesiveness—our last time of "WE." In the 1950s and early 1960s, it was easy to know where "WE" (a shared identity, public space, and a functioning common good) lived because "WE" was everywhere there were people. At least it was an ideological "WE" that spoke the language of "WE," even though it didn't fully include African Americans, Latinos, Asians, immigrants, and non-heterosexuals who were supposed to act like "WEs" while actually being required to live on the sidelines. Society-making media (as opposed to segment-making media) had the upper hand, but the way in which some groups were pushed aside is what Turrow referred to in the last chapter when he described society-making media as marginalizing some groups, stereotyping others, and presenting an overall picture of the world in a more ideal vision of the actual reality. Nonetheless, there was a clear recognizable "WE."

It was the era of broadcast technology. Like every earlier age shaped by the dominant technology of its time, the technology of broadcasting gave shape to the way in which people communicated, were educated, organized, and shaped community. Along with a shared post–World War

II identity, radio and broadcast TV, with their very limited but dominating offerings, helped make everyone a "WE." It was a time when the World Series was on TV and there was no ESPN to offer alternatives, no British Broadcasting to offer anything other than US sports, and no networks on Internet platforms singularly focused on basketball, football, or rugby no matter what the calendar-driven sport season might be. There was only the Major League Baseball World Series, and "WE" all watched it together. All the WE children watched *The Wonderful World of Disney* on Sunday nights as the weekend wound down before Monday school. With only three broadcast news stations, all "WEs" heard the same news stories that were different only in the personalities of, and the preferential loyalty of listeners to, the newscasters who told the stories. With only TV and radio providing limited, generalized offerings, but holding a large national platform, it was fairly easy for the mainline Protestant religion (the "established State religion") to find its best speakers and storytellers and give WE a regular dose of common good religion on national programs such as *The Protestant Hour*. Having only a few nationally dominant platforms with little diversity gave Protestantism a very large voice for "WE" to hear. "WE" was everywhere and quite easy to talk to.

So, given the present argument of now being a time of turning when the most recent dominant voice has been "I," what does it mean for the congregation to lean into the "WE"? In this time of the dominant I, the "WE" that is seeking to emerge is quite a bit more difficult to find and talk to. Where WE once lived with such high visibility and easy access in the 1950s, the people have now been divided into marketing subgroups, tribal subcultures, and Internet "communities" on multiple and micro-platforms with competing purposes and conversations. The move from the broadcast era to the time of digital, and then Internet technology, has changed again how people communicate, are educated, organize, and shape community. The "WE" has been divided and then subdivided into many multiple tribal gatherings of I's. Even "I" doesn't have to be unified anymore. With the new tools of technology, the individual can choose multiple personalities and avatars, being one person at home, another at work, and a far different person than either home or work while surfing the Internet. If the "WE" is to emerge again, it is beginning from a very different starting place.

Where can the congregation now take its treasure to support the resurging oscillation of the WE that is so needed for a more balanced, life-giving, future? What is clear is that the public space and the common good that is so essential to life, will come back, but it will return in some very different form(s) in this new iteration of our oscillating national history. It will not return by going back to what once was. To that point, congregations will not return to being natural gathering places of public space as they once were, which allowed them to practice the familiar old attractional ministry of calling increasing numbers of people into membership. The oscillating cultural values may be swinging back toward the "WE" that once was, but it will not be by familiar means returning to familiar forms.

Hope lies, as described in chapter 2, in congregations having the capacity to be malleable when the cultural context around them slowly and deeply changes. Finding new ways to share their ancient and valuable treasure of institutional values with a culture changing toward "WE" is within the reach of congregations. It was done in the past. This time, however, it will not rest on congregations picking up the same cultural roles that they currently know or remember from their recent past. The search for the necessary new roles for congregations in the changing American landscape will be the first steps toward the discovery of new organizational forms that congregations will need in order to live out their institutional purpose in a cultural setting that has changed once again. Leaders will now be required to ask the question identified earlier that does not yet have an answer—what now is a congregation?

The "WE" and the Neighborhood

It may be a paradox in a world that can be instantly global that the first new space for a turn toward the "WE" will be in the familiar area of the neighborhood—the actual geography in which the congregation naturally lives. The neighborhood space in which the institutional congregation will need to do its work of usufruct will heavily shape the new form and role that the congregation will need to create in the turning.

Many congregations have become accustomed to looking too far beyond their neighborhood for their voices to be heard and their influence to be felt. They may be participating in the large hashtag movements that now organize for social change. But this has more likely been the domain of Burton's civil religion of social justice where the church's voice was little heard while individuals pursued their own personal liberties of the self. Congregations may also be lending themselves to organized efforts to influence legislators to do what they believed to be the right thing, only to find that they have wandered into the domain of the institutions of the state where the voice of morality is little heard. Many congregations are working hard to learn their way onto the Internet, seeking to find new connections, relationships, and community. All of this has been worthy work in the political turmoil of the Internet age, but all of this work takes the attention of the congregation beyond its own physical neighborhood as if what needs to happen is "out there."

No doubt the notion of the work of the church as being out there came as a consequence of the congregation losing its own anchor in earlier established neighborhoods. As the post–World War II generation became increasingly mobile and suburbanized, more and more members relocated away from the physical neighborhood of their congregation. Yet they regularly drove back for Sunday worship and weekday meetings and programs. Having lost their immediate neighborhood connections, congregations learned how to leapfrog the space that closely surrounded them to stay connected to their more distant relocated members. They learned how to generalize their focus on the issues of the day instead of on the specific experience of the small patch of the mission field that most closely surrounded them. In the process, the neighborhood and the congregation separated ways, and the common good was less and less nurtured.

However, there is substantial evidence to suggest that the oscillation of values from the current "I" to the counterbalancing "WE" will not begin or initially thrive at the larger, regional, or global levels where other civil religions operate. The new forms of community and the common good are more likely to be birthed in the neighborhood in whatever shape the neighborhood takes, which is the best place in which to be a good neighbor.

The neighborhood is real space, it is real people, it is not conceptual. It is here, not out there. One of the distracting words that many congregations learned to use is "community," which can be used as a synonym for neighborhood. But *community* is a word with generic character different from the specificity of neighborhood. "The community" was the language often used by mission-minded congregations that felt led to make a difference in the world—out there. Such use of the notion of community is not dependent on location. It is not defined by specific people. Aspirational congregations quite often sought to be of service and ministry to "the community" by sending dollars, food, or other resources to people whom they never met, whose names they never came to know, and who live in places the congregants never visited. Congregations learned to participate in a comfortable transfer of resources rather than the more stressful but rich connection of relationships. Community was an idea that was easily aspirationalized and generalized, but safe. The neighborhood is quite different. The neighborhood is specific and requires actual relationships. The neighborhood is local, and local is where the cultural change oscillating toward "WE" will first happen.

Margaret Wheatly has been spending her life caring about the world and how people live in it. It has brought her to the conclusion that what the world most needs now are local leaders. Change will not be brought by global leaders even though the world has become more and more global. Local leaders, not global. She argues that at one time, regional and global leaders did have the knowledge, technology, and tools to address the problems that were being encountered at global levels. However, they lacked the will to move to action because of the perceived cost of that action. Global poverty and hunger, climate change, war and gun violence, and human rights were once addressable on the larger scale. But, she writes this:

Now it is too late. We cannot solve these global issues globally. We can see them clearly. We can understand their root causes. We have evidence of solutions that would have solved them. But we refused to

compromise, to collaborate, to persevere in resolving them as an intel-
ligent, creative species living on one precious planet.

Now it is up to us, not as global leaders but as local leaders.[1]

Compromise, collaboration, and perseverance happen best at the local level because they are dependent on relationships. This is the domain of the institutions of morality. And they are what the institutions of morality do best.

Repeating again: What the institutions of the state and the economy do is competition and contest. Competition and contest are dependent upon power, not relationships. Here again, the shift from the broadcast age to the digital age to the Internet age has had its impact as the technology of our communication has reformed how we learn, how we organize, how we form community. This shift has changed the gathering and use of power. Moisés Naím argues that at one time the agents of power were primarily large governments and large corporations. The dominating institutions of the state and the economy. They exercised power by setting up boundaries that other smaller and different voices could not breach, but this monopoly over power was changed in the age of the Internet when formerly established boundaries of all natures were digitally crossed easily and swiftly. In the new age of the Internet and digital technology, power has shifted to the small and nimble. But Naím argues that power, which has been increasingly easy to access, has become increasingly difficult to use.[2] The consequence of such deep digital shifts to the essential nature and use of power at the regional and global levels now leads to gridlock. As the traditional large agents of power compete with each other while simultaneously trying to stave off the new, small, nimble, tech-smart agents of power, the contest over power now leads to stalemate and the inability to act. Consider the United States Congress and its inability to pass legislation as a highly public example. The most fertile soil for change is no longer in the hands of the large agents; it is now in the hands of the small at the local level. For the congregation, it is found in the neighborhood.

Living in the Changed Neighborhood

In earlier times, the congregation was a primary gathering place at the neighborhood level. Across its various historic forms as described by Holifield in chapter 2, the congregation retained the function of being an "extrafamilial form of community"—a gathering place outside the family. During the colonial period, it was "comprehensive" (i.e., the only gathering place in town). In the devotional period at the turn of the nineteenth century, it began its segmented form, separately serving the divisions of the public that were being shaped by race, ethnicity, and economics. Nonetheless, it was still a primary gathering place for each segment of the public it served. As social congregations in the late nineteenth and early-twentieth century, the congregation was not only a gathering place but also a service provider to the slice or segment of the public to which it related. And in its participatory role in the mid to late-twentieth century, it performed its gathering function by being the suburban landing place for that part of the population that was mobile and the anchoring place of security for those remaining in the city. What was consistent through the multiple historic roles of the American congregation was its service as a gathering place in the neighborhood.

The difference today is that people do not gather in the same or similar ways as they did in the past. The neighborhood today is quite different in the twenty-first century because technology has provided a way for people to gather without regard to geography. Here, we will turn primarily to the work of Marc Dunkelman to help understand that our culture is now seeking to reclaim "WE" values, while both the neighbors and the neighborhoods so closely connected to "WE" have essentially vanished.

One of the streams of influence to vanishing neighborhoods has been the strong cultural emphasis on the individual. Well within the theme of "self" that has been central to my argument in this book, Dunkelman writes, "Americans of all stripes have been given a license to abandon the relationships that don't interest them for those that do; we have been given the opportunity to pick and choose the relationships we most want to maintain."[3] This is the moral polestar social contract at work on the relational level. Neighbors, friends, and relationships are free to be chosen based on their contributions to the preferences and needs of the individuals. The present focus on the individual has, itself, changed the neighborhood.

If one stream of influence that changed the neighborhood is the individualism of the culture, the second contributing stream of influence has been the shift to the Internet and its digital technology as the dominant tool of communication. As described earlier, new communication platforms and their tools change the very way in which we order our lives—and in this case the tools most at hand creating change have been the computer, the electronic tablet, and the cell phone.

Dunkelman uses the well-established anthropologic construct of the "social brain hypothesis" developed by Robin Dunbar at Oxford.[4] In this construct, the emergence of humans as the most powerful species hinged on their ability to communicate. As brains got bigger and information and networks of relationships became more complex, humans developed critical schemes of organization. The need to manage an increasing number of relationships and the limit of the size and capability of the human brain forced humans to group their relationships. What emerged from Dunbar's research was the systematic way in which every society utilizes

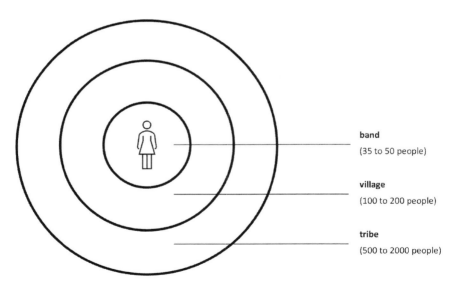

band
(35 to 50 people)

village
(100 to 200 people)

tribe
(500 to 2000 people)

Figure 7.1. Social Brain Hypothesis

a three-category structure of group relationships: bands, villages, and tribes, as seen in figure 7.1.

Looking outward from the perspective of the individual, the first and smaller circle, which is the *band*, consists of the roughly thirty-five to fifty people that an individual knows best, is most intimate with in their sharing, and most frequently engages in direct relationship. These are the family members, friends, and work colleagues whose names and stories are intimately known and who make up the bulk of an individual's daily relational contacts.

The next circle out in distance from the individual is the *village*. The village is a gathering of people of about 100 to 200 in number, which may consist of a network of bands with special ties to one another. One might not personally know everyone in the village, but certainly one would know someone else who did know the other people until the village is a network of people who are all connected. The village is a gathering of people who interact sufficiently on a daily basis to develop strong bonds based on direct personal contact. If the band is one's circle of family and friends, the village is one's neighborhood. It certainly contains a diversity of people both like and unlike any single individual in the village. Relationships are not determined by similarity or agreeability, but by proximity and connections to other village residents. This is the neighborhood that has been disappearing in America over past decades, and it lives at the local level—as distinct from the intimate level of the band or the nongeographic level of the tribe.

The *tribe* is a grouping of people numbering from 500 to 2,000, who are connected, not by direct relationship but by shared common traditions such as language, rituals, or interests. The tribe commonly consists of groupings of multiple villages. It does not depend upon personal connection but on shared traditions and convictions.

Given the three rings of band, village, and tribe, it is the middle ring of the village that is important for our understanding of what has happened to our neighborhood. Dunkelman describes the village in this way:

Middle-ring relationships are defined by a familiarity that allows acquaintances to carry on conversations about personal subjects even

*if they aren't entirely private: the birth of a child, for example, an
ongoing illness, or a funny coincidence from a few years back. They
represent, in essence, the people with whom an individual is familiar
but not intimate, friendly but not close.[5]*

Over time, Dunkelman points out, this middle ring became what Americans consider "community"—what I am referring to as "neighborhood." It is geographic and clearly connected—"not as close as kith or kin, but not as distant as a mere acquaintance."[6]

It is this neighborhood over the past recent decades that has been disappearing.

CAUSES FOR THE DISAPPEARING NEIGHBORHOOD

The disappearance of the middle circle of neighborhood can be explained by pointing to so very many seemingly unrelated changes that have accumulated over past decades. The development of the American highway system allowed people to live in places where they did not work, which then required commuting, which then reduced the time and energy available to visit neighbors and be involved in neighborhood activities. The advent of TV and air conditioning took people off of their porches and moved them inside of their homes. Consequently, front porch sitting and after dinner walks in which one would encounter neighbors disappeared. Eventually, the design of suburban homes replaced the front porch of the home with a back deck, which, if one did to choose to sit outside, would again reduce neighborly connection since out of sight means out of mind. The very ways in which we continually adjusted our daily living was increasingly unneighborly.

Returning to the issue of communication and technology we can further see how deeply embedded our dismissal of the middle ring of the neighborhood has become. The cell phone is the best example because it is connected to both cellular and Internet communication systems and it is ubiquitous—we don't go anywhere without it. More important, cell phones are connected to the inner circle of the band. The names, phone numbers, and personal information of the thirty-five to fifty people in an individual's band are all in the cell phone's contact app, and the most significant of them are electronically starred to provide instant calling. While the promise of mobile technology was described as a direct connection to an ever-widening world, studies show that the majority of cell phone conversations actually go to the closest three to five relationships in a person's band (i.e., not to the wider world, but to the most relational world).[7] Used as a telephone, the cell phone is clearly an instrument of the inner circle of the band. In a very fast-paced world, it keeps the bonds of intimate relationship strong and supple within the band.

But if the cell phone serves the small inner band, it also gives us mobile, continuous, connection to the Internet where the third circle of the tribe lives. It is on the Internet where the people of the current "I" culture have learned to create and curate their own personal tribes. This is contemporary life in the outer circle where people bookmark whatever particular news feed they find to be most personally satisfying and reinforcing to the tribe of similar people that they fashion for themselves. The Internet is where the individual checks in on the tribe that speaks his or her chosen "language" that is connected to preferred interests—perhaps the tribe of amateur photographers, or the tribe of those who can't stop watching cat videos, or the tribe that speaks the language of baseball statistics, or the tribe that follows and catalogues the sins, lies, and conspiracies committed by the Republicans, Democrats, Libertarians, Antifa, the Far Right, and so forth (this one is multiple choice with something for everyone's tribe).

The cell phone that is the ubiquitous instrument of the inner circle of the band also serves the outer circle of the tribe as well. It seems as if the "self" in the present "I" age has found a connection between these two circles. The band and the tribe have some previously undiscovered similarities in the Internet age, which are related to the ways in which each provide affirmation to the individual. As Dunkelman explains,

> *No one doubts that there's a world of difference between our most and least intimate connections. But bonds formed between dear friends and near strangers can sometimes scratch the same itch. Indeed, if there's an alternative place in the constellation of rings where someone might find the same element of affirmation, it's the outer rings [the*

ring of the band and the ring of the tribe]. One-dimensional relation-ships that connect individuals on nothing more than a single plane of mutual interest—those formed between political junkies, hobbyists, and sport fans, for example—can often cultivate the same kind of validation. And, for that reason, Americans have become increasingly inclined to seek them out.[8]

Once again, it is the middle ring that is left out and the neighborhood goes unnourished. This is simply daily life in the Internet age, which is now second nature to us.

To use a simple example of the vanishing neighborhood, consider something as common as my grandchildren's community soccer games. When the soccer game is being played, to be sure, all eyes are on the field and the children. There is very little relational connection happening on the sidelines during the game as spectators follow every kick and encour-agingly yell to players to run faster and with more persistence than the adults themselves ever ran as a child. But then comes halftime. One of three things then happen on the sideline as the play comes to a stop.

1. Adults quickly cluster in conversations with others that are already in their inner circle band. These are close friends who also have a child on the team or are already part of one another's daily or regular connections through work or school, or perhaps their own parents who came to watch grandchildren play, just as my wife and I did. Or, for the next two options, cell phones come out.

2. The cell phones are used to connect with other inner circle members of the person's band who are not present at the game—perhaps checking to see if children at home have completed assigned chores, or checking with close friends to confirm the time of the dinner at a restaurant that evening.

3. Alternately, the cell phones are used not to connect with the inner circle of the band, but to the outer circle of the individual's curated tribe—catching up with the final score and stats from last night's pro game, scrolling through Facebook postings, checking

the preferred newsfeed to see the latest on what former president Trump did yesterday or what was done to him.

The cell phone serves both the band and the tribe as an instrument of relationship or connection. What is not served is the neighborhood. The conversation that does not happen with frequency on the halftime side-line of a community soccer game is the one that connects people across the most local of geographies to build up public space and the common good: "Hi, how are you? I don't recognize you; do you live around here? Which one of the kids is yours?"

People Still Live There

If the neighborhood has disappeared, people still live where it once was. It's just that the people living there don't know each other.

In their book on the art of neighboring, Jay Pathak and Dave Runyon offer an exercise in which an individual divides a piece of paper into a 3 x 3 grid of nine boxes in which the center box represents his or her own home.[9] (See figure 7.2.)

The other eight boxes surrounding the center HOME box represent the nearest homes in the neighborhood surrounding his or her own. The

1	2	3
4	HOME	5
6	7	8

Figure 7.2. The Neighborhood

individual is then asked to complete their answers to a set of three questions for each of the eight surrounding homes:

a. Write the names of the people who live in the house represented by the box. If you can give first and last names, that's great. If only the first names, that's fine too.

b. Write down some relevant information about each person, some data or facts about him or her that you couldn't see just by standing in your driveway, things you might know if you've spoken to the person once or twice.

c. Write down some in-depth information you would know after connecting with people. This might include career plans or dreams of starting a family or anything to do with the purpose of their lives—something meaningful you've learned through interacting with them.

Having used this exercise with a good number of people, Pathak and Runyon report the following results:

- About 10 percent of people can fill out the names of all eight of their neighbors, question a.
- About 3 percent of the people can fill out question b for every home.
- Less than 1 percent can fill out responses for question c for every home.

This is not the neighborhood that many leaders in congregations remember, and it is certainly not the neighborhood that once shaped the role of the local organizational congregation. It is also not a neighborhood that will nostalgically reappear in the process of a cultural turning. Organizational congregations will not do well to assume that people will return to a time in which they will naturally seek out established neighborhood congregations for worship, relationships, programs, or support for their lives. Neighborhoods no longer have natural neighbors.

People Still Live There—and There Is Ferment Afoot

Where once there used to be a neighborhood, there are now residences. Where once there used to be congregations that served as natural neighborhood gathering places, there are now buildings that attract a continually decreasing percentage of Americans who may or may not know each other well. Indeed, congregations are becoming invisible neighbors on the landscape themselves. A consultant colleague of mine was once asked to work with a congregation in New York City that was concerned about its declining membership and presence in the city. The congregation was housed in a massive stone building on a very busy downtown street corner where thousands of people passed by each day. To get very basic feedback from the people surrounding the church, the consultant simply stood at the bus stop that was on the very corner of where the church building was located. He asked people waiting at the bus stop a very simple question: "Can you direct me to the nearest church?" To the congregation's dismay, most people pointed away from the corner, offering directions that would take the consultant blocks away from the imposing church building in the shadow of which the people were talking. Buildings unused, like neighbors not spoken to, seem to simply disappear.

FERMENT AND EXPERIMENTATION

This is not news that surprises. Denominational leaders and researchers have been tracking the impact of these trends for some time. But what also needs to be said is that there is a good amount, and an increasing amount, of ferment and experimentation by established leaders and congregations seeking to learn new ways to live in places that no longer function as neighborhoods once did. There is also a new burst of entrepreneurial experiments in which people have already risked and invested themselves in finding ways to help the values of the institutional church live in their own neighborhoods. It is all work that offers a leading edge to understand what the organizational congregation will need to address in order to accommodate and thrive in the future. The two foundations to which my own work is most closely connected have invested deeply in understanding and encouraging this work of experimentation and learning: The Texas Methodist Foundation (https://tmf -fdn.org/leadership-ministry) and the Wesleyan Impact Parters (https:// www.wesleyanimpactpartners.org). An Internet search of sites connected to Fresh Expressions and The Neighboring Movement will also offer portals into the early stages of how the church is learning to live in a turning culture. And, of course, the very nature of the Internet allows one to start in any place, such as those noted here, and begin a trail that will lead to more and more efforts, experiments, and examples based on new learning.

It is not the purpose of this book to walk into the experimentation already being done. This is rich work being done by courageous leaders willing to step out from the safety and security of already established organizational institutions. The work is still in early stages, the learning of transitive effort that happens between what was and what is not yet. Nonetheless, guiding lights are beginning to appear that should capture and guide the attention of others.

For example, Blair Thompson-White has been walking alongside creative leaders and courageous entrepreneurs in her role as director of Leadership Ministry at The Texas Methodist Foundation. In her engagement and interviews with these leaders, she offers three early guiding stars from this new, young work for others to follow.[10] The first guiding star she identified is "follow what makes you come alive." Mission, ministry, and change follows energy. Where the established organizational congregation has been losing energy along with other precious resources by doing what is normative and what is expected of the established organizational congregation for too long, Blair offers an example of how important it is to follow the conviction that God calls people and institutions to do something about what motivates them most. The second insight is to "pursue new questions." Talking to the same people about the same questions results in the same answers. The new leaders and entrepreneurs ask different questions as well as familiar questions intentionally twisted into new shapes. Pointing to the work of Shannon Hopkins and the Fresh Expressions movement, Blair points to an old question such as,

"How do we get more people in the pews on Sunday morning?" and the difference a new question would make, such as, "What are the spiritual needs of those who will never darken the doors of the church?" Such new questions provide very different paths to follow. These are paths that may not yet have clear answers, but don't so quickly run off into the roadblocks and dead ends of the old, familiar questions of diminishing organizational congregations. And then the third insight: "discover your neighbor's gifts." Now, we are back to the neighborhood again as the locus of ministry, the level at which change toward the common good will most easily emerge, and the territory that the congregation knows best. Consider the significant difference that the turning of a culture and the loss of the neighborhood means. None of the three questions lead anywhere near to the older north star that congregations once used to guide them to connections with others: "find a need and fill it." New days require new questions; a new wilderness requires a different north star.

THE NEW ROLE AND FORM OF USUFRUCT

What institutions do most importantly is usufruct. There are valuable life-giving narratives, guiding-light values, and well-known behaviors and practices that bring meaning and purpose to living and which equip people to live together with one another. This is the work of the institutions of morality, which must constantly adapt their cultural role and their organizational form over time to function as needed. The work of usufruct requires institutions to be steady in purpose but flexible in role and form. The treasure that the institutional congregation holds, and the importance of practicing usufruct, is not in question at all. It is the role and form of the congregation that must now be questioned, made malleable, and risk being countercultural.

CHAPTER 8

Jesus Is Enough

ALTHOUGH ST. PAUL DID NOT FOUND THE CONGREGATION AT COLOS-sae, he had a deep connection to the people and listened closely to the news that reached him from there. What he heard about that congregation was people contesting with each other over the use of distinctly Jewish practices in search of special knowledge. It seems as if the people were fussing with each other about how to be Christian. Perhaps there are just some arguments that are ageless. In writing to the Colossians, Paul offered his own response to the reports that reached him. It was a response so ageless that I find myself sitting up at attention because of what I have been describing beginning in chapter 1: the civil religions of social justice, techno-utopianism, and atavism; the self-serving worship of consumerism; the temptations of tribal communities all arguing competitively for people to follow their truth. If the Colossians argued about how to see and how to be in the world, then we are the timeless extension of that same argument that won't go away. In what feels like real prescience, Paul wrote,

> See to it that nobody enslaves you with philosophy and foolish deception, which conforms to human traditions and the way the world thinks and acts rather than Christ. (Colossians 2:8)

In response to their competing arguments, Paul simply reminded the Colossians that Jesus was enough. They were already baptized in Jesus (2:12). They already had a sense of new life (2:13). They were already forgiven (2:13). The record of past debts that constrained them was already destroyed (2:14). The secular rulers and authorities that lorded over them were already exposed as empty (2:15). Paul was saying that all those arguments in which others judge you for your religious practices and your worldview are over. All that competition from those who want to sell you their truth about how the world works is null and void. Jesus is enough.

As I have been arguing here, the alternative narrative of truth that is held by the congregation offers an end to the competition and gridlock about power and resources that now hold our world near crisis. Learning how to love God is enough because we are all made by the same hand and all share the same creation. Being a good neighbor—loving others as you love yourself—is enough, because we are all interdependent in this life together. Inviting everyone to the table, no matter their status or differences, is enough because we live in a world of sufficiency where everyone is sacred, and no one needs to be seen as taking anything away from others. This is how Jesus, son of God, saw the world. And Jesus is enough.

The way ahead in a gridlocked world, as shaped by the Christian worldview, is simple enough without being simplistic or Pollyannish. But it will take a good bit of deep behavioral discipleship to make our world different. As an American people, we are truly in a difficult spot—at the end of our cultural rope.

Of great importance is the reality that we now live in a time in which there are no agreed-upon rules. We are a-nomos, according to Walter Brueggemann—living in a time without norms. As congregations seek a way forward, it is critical to understand the pervasiveness of a normless time and the difficulty that living without norms and consensual rules creates. Currently, a-nomos is so pervasive that we hardly notice it and therefore don't factor it into our hopes and actions in the world. But consider—recently, my wife, Lynne, and I were invited to a celebration meal of sixteen people that was hosted at a very upscale restaurant. Quite naturally, our conversation turned to what was appropriate for us to wear to such an event in such a place. So, Lynne turned to our son for advice since he has worked in the hospitality industry for years and is very familiar with the current restaurant scene. To the question of what is appropriate to wear to an upscale restaurant, he wisely answered that we should dress for the group of people that we would be with for the evening, not for the restaurant in which we would be hosted. He said that no matter how upscale a restaurant might be, there would be no dress code observed by the patrons. People come as they wish when living in a time of a-nomos. And indeed, as we entered the restaurant all dressed up for our celebrating group, we saw others in everything from dressy casual to beach wear. A simple example of no norms.

Or consider—not long ago, Lynne and I were driving along a commercial street in Northwest Philadelphia on a Saturday afternoon, and we were surrounded by five young men on noisy motorbikes. They popped wheelies while surrounding us, wove in and out, back and forth around us, crossing traffic lanes in front of oncoming cars, and darted through intersections ignoring red lights. My hands were grasping the steering wheel through all of it, while they were quite clearly just out for an afternoon's (dangerous) fun. They gave no considerations to norms—not even those that rise to the level of rules and laws meant to protect them and others—doing only what was fun in their eyes. We can all add to the increasing number of norms being disregarded that range from the annoying (people with thirty grocery items in the checkout lane designated for ten items or less) to the unthinkable (children carrying guns to school to address hurt feelings with violence).

We live in a time in which competing worldviews and the intensity of individual freedoms of an "I" culture have abrogated many earlier established norms, rules, laws, and agreements that guide safe and respectful ways for people to live together. From dress codes and traffic laws, the progression of examples of a-nomos leads as far as ignoring the norms of democracy at the time of a peaceful transfer of power in a presidential election, or as far as one nation ignoring global treaties that prohibit attacks on another nation. The return to a time of civility, the recapturing of the common good, and reinstilling a sense of shared humanity will not be an easy task for the institutions of morality in a time of a-nomos when there is no line too sacred to be crossed.

So here we are deeply embedded in a moment of cultural chaos, and within the institutional congregation there is a way for us, as groups, communities, and as a nation to move ahead together. Jesus is enough. This treasure held by the congregation is countercultural, which is just what is most needed when everything around us is stuck. The competing cultural and tribal messages currently claiming attention have led us to gridlock and a-nomos, while around us all is changing. The competing messages of an "I" culture, too long embraced, have brought us to an unsafe space where, in the name of liberty, guns are more valued than children's lives. We have been led to tribal disagreements that have escalated from the battle of words to the use of weapons. Thanks be to God that the congregation is countercultural because something different desperately needs to be heard. Being countercultural does not mean that the congregation is disconnected from the culture. It means that the congregation, now perhaps more than at other times, has something different to say.

TELL US HOW

If the argument is as I have offered, the next natural question that leaders ask is what should congregations *do*? If the congregation is to speak, how do leaders rebuild individual and community trust in congregations? How do congregations gain their place in new forms of neighborhood? How do religious leaders get out from under their organizational stresses in order to have a word of hope for the larger community in which they live? How does the congregation attract the attention of younger generations in order to share their treasure? How do existing congregations repurpose themselves, gather more members, find more resources, fill their buildings, regain their public voice? The list of questions goes on at some length.

There are two sets of answers. One answer is, "We don't know." The other answer is, "We know quite a lot."

Answer #1: We Don't Know

There is no shame in leaders of congregations not knowing clearly how to right all that has felt wrong. In his history of humankind, Yuval Harari pointedly states that modern science is based on the Latin injunction *ignoramus*—"we do not know."[1] The only way to move ahead is to assume that we don't already know everything. He points out that premodern map makers drew complete world maps long before they were familiar with the entire globe. Unknown spaces were filled with the images of monsters and wonders, as if map makers did know what was out there, giving the sense of a world understood. Such maps did not stir up the spirit of wonder and exploration but rather kept people at home in their known places and familiar ways out of fear of what they saw on the maps. Harari points out that it was during the fifteenth and sixteenth centuries that map makers began to draw world maps with lots of empty spaces.[2] The empty spaces were a breakthrough, an acknowledgment of what was not known—*ignoramus*. It was a turning point toward a time of exploration, beginning with Christopher Columbus sailing west from Spain in 1492 to disprove what he assumed and to discover what he didn't know.

Congregations and their leaders are in such a time of *ignoramus*. Understandably, most of the questions that haunt leaders in congregations are organizational in nature. How do they now revitalize, resource, energize, provide leadership for, gain market share for the established religious organizations dotting the landscape that have been struggling through the decades of the "I" culture? Importantly, these questions must be recognized as organizational rather than institutional questions given the distinction offered in chapter 4. It has been an exceedingly difficult time for organizational religion during the "I" time in which congregations were not trusted, in which individuals did not join membership-based organizations, and in which the jurisdiction that once belonged to the institutions of morality was so eagerly outsourced to the state and to the economy.

If all that leaders are going to ask are organizational questions, it may be an indication that we are still looking for completed maps—as if what we are looking for is somewhere known by someone. If leaders are finding some answers for themselves to any of the many organizational questions, even partial answers, then they should move ahead with what they see. Moving toward organizational answers will undoubtedly help all of us to learn more in this liquid cultural time. But the reality is that we do not, with any conviction, know. *Ignoramus*.

But be quick to note that this ignorance is widespread beyond congregations. Postpandemic businesses and corporations do not yet know how to effectively construct an in-person/home-office work force for the next age of employment. With the increasingly unbearable weight of the cost of education, universities do not yet know how to balance the social learning necessary to young adulthood, with the teacher-student relationship, with the increasing growth of information in digital form, with the technology that is redefining both communication and community gathering space—all into a mode of learning that will be affordable, provide personal maturity, support future employment, teach people the art of thinking, and lead toward wisdom. No matter where one looks it is easy to see what is not known and, in every case, how the future of organizational life is complex and confusing. Congregations are far from alone both in their anxiety over the present and their ignorance about the future.

A good part of the reason that leaders cast about looking for advice telling them what to do instead of settling into the hard personal work of learning is because we all underestimate the depth of change that we now face. As an American people, we are not just confronted with the changes prompted by technology, political populism, or the aftermath of a global pandemic—as daunting as any or all of these challenges may be. We are at the same time in the deeper, quieter, and much more demanding cyclical, oscillating turning of an era. I noted briefly in chapter 3, the importance of a cyclical understanding of history—the perspective that history does indeed repeat itself in its cyclical attention to some values over others—in its use of heroes at some points and its use of disrupters at others, in its oscillating preference of either individualism or the common good. Strauss and Howe identify four repeating cycles of history that humans have followed for centuries and have identified them as repeating turnings of eras *[with my bracketed interpretation]*:

- The *First Turning* is a *High*, an upbeat era of strengthening institutions and weakening individualism, when a new civic order implants and the old values regime decays. *[Consider our own era of post-World War II cohesion.]*

- The *Second Turning* is an *Awakening*, a passionate era of spiritual upheaval, when the civic order comes under attack from a new values regime. *[Consider our own era of the youth rebellion of the 1960s.]*

- The *Third Turning* is an *Unraveling*, a downcast era of strengthening individualism and weakening institutions, when the old civic order decays and the new values regime implants. *[Consider our own era of 1980s greed and 2000s political gridlock.]*

- The *Fourth Turning* is a *Crisis*, a decisive era of secular upheaval, when the values regime propels the replacement of the old civic order with a new one.[3] *[Consider that this is where we are now.]*

The impulses attached to each of these turnings shift with the appearance of each changing era. In the first Turning the impulse is to *belong*, in the second to *defy*, in the third to *separate*, and in the fourth to *gather*.[4] As an American people we have progressed sufficiently in our cycle of upheaval that there is a new impulse mounting to find ways to reclaim a common order. We are trying to gather again. A thorough telling of American history from the end of World War II to the present day, as done by Strauss and Howe, brings life to these cyclical turnings in easily recognizable form to anyone who has lived through any part of the last eighty years.

In this book I have primarily been examining our recent experience of the Third Turning with its attention to individualism and the weakening of institutions. But as an American people we are already actively entering into the Fourth Turning, which is a time of crisis. Strauss and Howe describe Fourth Turnings as an "era of maximum darkness, in which the supply of social order is still falling but the demand for order is now rising."[5] It takes some form of crisis or crises in every Fourth Turning for a people to begin to mobilize toward a new order. Americans have now been mounting and layering their crises over recent years as energy builds up for something new—crises such as the post-modern break in our trust of science, to the rebirth of rampant racism, white supremacy, and nationalism, to the global dissolution of international alliances and treaties that destabilizes all nations.

While the energy that comes in a time of crisis is high and people battle willingly over the changes they seek, it remains difficult for leaders to know how to prepare for the future. Increasingly, organizations, including congregations, know that they must change substantively. But there is no clear direction, and certainly no consensus, for leaders to follow. A major contributor to the lack of clarity is that, if Strauss and Howe's description is helpful, we are in a Fourth Turning seeking a way to return to another First Turning—the next First Turning of a historically repeating cycle. We are seeking to begin again, just as so many other generations did when they too "ran out of rope," as described in chapter 3. We are seeking to get back to a time of a new civic order that will return us to stronger institutions and weakened individualism. *But that is just the point which creates our blind ignorance of how to quickly change our organizations to meet this new era. We are not going back to an earlier First Turning. We are not returning to anything we have known. We are instead moving somewhat blindly ahead toward a new First Turning whose shape and form is not yet know*n. While the impulses and the values of the four-cycle Turnings repeat, the form, structure, behaviors, norms, practices, and information is never replicated in known, recognizable ways. On the cusp of a cultural shift, we are already a people deeply changed by technology, a digital existence, and the connectedness of global communication. We are already a different people living in patterns unknown to our past. What we are seeking in terms of gathering, community, and values has been pursued before. But what we still need to learn about how to structure that gathering and community, shape those values, and form a new social contract has not been seen before. We are truly at that moment of crossing the bridge while building it. So, yes. We do not know. How could we?

Perhaps the part of our ignorance that so exhausts our clergy and lay leaders is the tempting allure of a nostalgia of certainty that still plays in the minds of those who remember an earlier time and believe we can return to it. It is both exhausting and personally dangerous for clergy and lay leaders to explore what is not yet understood if they are in a place where they are constantly reminded of, evaluated by, and rewarded according to a nostalgically remembered time when congregations were once naturally strong in an environment that welcomed and supported institutional organizations. Nostalgia tempts us into thinking that we do know how things should be and what we should do. After all, we did it before and it worked.

In an earlier book, *Quietly Courageous,* I pointed out the three temptations of nostalgia: (1) it gives us only a one-sided story to live, (2) it invites us to rest on past diagnoses, and (3) it allows us to avoid difficult questions about the present and future.[6] Nostalgia keeps us stuck in ignorance rather than using ignorance to move us ahead. What we do not know in the present moment is not always a problem to solve. It is, however, the condition under which we must learn to live while seeking our future. Relaxing into what we do not know can energize us to use what we are learning about the future, and of this new learning and the future we do know quite a lot.

Answer #2: We Know Quite a Lot

What we do know is that our world is now out of balance, which requires resilience, not certainty, in order to live. There are some congregations and some leaders who are learning to be resilient. What we do know is that riding the current cultural wave has been teaching congregations some fundamental necessities that we have yet to figure out how to operationalize as religious organizations. Among them are how to be the following:

1. Participants rather than providers

2. Platforms rather than gathering places

3. Plain speakers rather than jargon junkies

Let's begin with resilience and the unusual opportunity of a hinge moment.

Living in a Hinge Moment—Resilience and Possibility

If all that I have written about the culture and the congregation here feels like chaos, that is a good thing. Chaos may be confusing and exhausting, but it is an environment of great portent and possibility. Chaos is the condition out of which new things are birthed. As a fan of Michael Crichton's writing (and the Jurassic Park movies that came from his novels), let's turn to the character of Dr. Malcolm, who is the voice of systems theory in *The Lost World*, Crichton's novel of prehistoric dinosaurs that are reclaimed and cloned from ancient DNA to live in a contemporary jungle. Malcolm describes chaos and the rich possibility that comes to those who risk choosing to live on the edge. This is not as far of a jump as some might at first think. Religious organizations are now trying to figure out how their own ancient DNA can be given new life in a present and future cultural jungle that has not been experienced before. Malcolm's description is a system's perspective that belongs as much to congregations as to any and all living systems.

> *Complex systems tend to locate themselves at a place we call "the edge of chaos." We imagine the edge of chaos as a place where there is enough innovation to keep a living system vibrant, and enough stability to keep it from collapsing into anarchy. It is a zone of conflict and upheaval, where the old and the new are constantly at war. Finding the balance point must be a delicate matter—if a living system drifts too close, it risks falling over into incoherence and dissolution; but if the system moves too far away from the edge, it becomes rigid, frozen, totalitarian. Both conditions lead to extinction. Too much change is as destructive as too little. Only at the edge of chaos can complex systems flourish.[7]*

Living at the edge of chaos is indeed a balancing act, but it allows leaders to use the advantage of a hinge moment such as a cultural turning of values. Importantly, to live at the edge of chaos requires, above all else, resilience.

Bishop Janice Riggle Huie has begun the important work of understanding resilience in our religious systems. Out of a spirit of hope and courage she writes of the "privilege of living at a hinge moment in history."[8] A hinge moment is an in-between time. It is an in-between political time such as living in the space between January 6 and January 20, 2021, not knowing what kind of a nation we will choose to be. It is living between the push for racial justice and the resurgence of white racism not knowing what kind of people we will choose to be. At the center of the argument that I have been framing in this book, it is living between the individual values of "I" and the common good values of "WE" not knowing in which direction we will choose to lean in order to shape the cultural chapter we next need as Americans.

Hinge moments come at the point of a "threshold" in systems change. Huie notes that giving attention to a threshold is key to developing resilience:

> *Thresholds are the point where a system has changed so substantively that it transitions into an entirely different regime. Knowing where thresholds might lie and being attentive to the drivers that cause it to cross into an alternative reality is critical to resilience thinking. The closer to a threshold, the less change is required to cross over to it.*[9]

A threshold and the edge of chaos have much in common. Both are the product of the tension and energy of something about to happen, as unpredictable as that "something" might be. The privilege of a threshold is that a change can be intentionally influenced without an excessive expense of energy because the system is already poised for change. Ours is clearly the hinge moment of a cultural turning as described above. As uncomfortable as it is to live and to seek to lead at such a time, we are nonetheless at the gateway to the next chapter of our history together as Americans and as Christians. Even a small push from congregations and the institutions of morality will have a significant impact.

The privilege of this hinge moment sitting at the threshold of a cultural systems shift is that the congregation can have both a voice and a role in the future that we will choose to live as an American people. Where the organizational congregation has most recently felt marginalized during a time when all institutions of morality have lost their voice, the culture is now at a threshold in which it can be influenced by the voices once pushed aside. It is time for the church to speak clearly, persuasively, and with courage from its countercultural position. It is a moment for congregations to push their anxieties aside and to speak clearly of the treasure they hold. The future depends upon it.

Resilience is the means by which one lives in a hinge moment—at the edge of chaos, neither too far into a change that causes dissolution, nor too far away from change that causes rigidity. At its most fundamental, resilience depends upon *identity* and *purpose*. "Ecologists define resilience as the capacity of a system to absorb disturbance and reorganize so that it retains its core purpose and identity in the face of dramatically changed circumstances."[10] Absorb disturbance (confusion, chaos, complexity, competition, simplistic nihilisms), yet retain its core purpose and identity. A systems rule of thumb states that in times of change, systems must be *steady in purpose but flexible in strategy*. Leaders of congregations may not be clear about what to do, but they must be tenaciously clear about who and why they are. Religious institutions in this hinge moment must be steady in identity and purpose—in usufruct. This is the treasure of the religious worldview with its disciplines and practices brought from the past, to help in the present, and to be made available for the future. While steadfast in their identity and purpose of usufruct, they must be equally flexible in their forms and strategies to engage a dramatically changed environment.

The threshold change to our values and behavior—which is now in the balance—will first appear at the local level. Regional, national, and global arenas are in permanent gridlock. The good news is that the local level is, at its most basic, the neighborhood, which is where congregations live. However, the congregation, which has historically always been a natural gathering place for the neighborhood must now face the challenge of fulfilling its identity and purpose in a neighborhood without neighbors and with people who now gather without regard for geography. Steady in identity and purpose, to be sure. Courageously seeking new strategies is the next step. For the ordained and lay leaders of institutional congregations, this is a straightforward issue of clarity and courage. Can leaders identify and claim the clear life-giving simplicity on which they stand as the holders of religious truth? Can they speak convincingly from their countercultural position about common good things that people have never stopped seeking? But can they also be courageously inventive?

Even as more cultural space is opening up in a threshold moment to give room to the usufruct of the congregation, strategies for how to be a congregation and how to live in the new neighborhood will need to be increasingly inventive and entrepreneurial.

Riding the Cultural Wave—Learning How to Resemble the Environment

We began with resilience to describe the considerable amount of what we already know about institutions living into the next era in America. We are also learning some rudimentary fundamentals about how our organizational institutions will need to restructure themselves in order to fulfill their identity and purpose in a changed environment. And here, as countercultural as the congregation may be at the moment, the challenge will be not in standing apart but rather fitting into the neighborhood. Over twenty years ago, Robert Wuthnow offered his study about the fragmentation of American communities. Early on in that work he wrote that "over a period of years, the organizations that manage to carve out a niche for themselves and are able to extract resources from their environment will not only survive but also come to resemble particular features of their environment."[11] The way to fit into the new neighborhood where the real change will come from is to find critical ways in which to resemble it. Here, I want to point to three modes of resemblance that we know of.

The first way requires congregations to understand themselves as *participants* rather than *provider*. The role of provider came easily enough to congregations in the post–World War II years since providing is connected to resources. As noted earlier, the postwar years in America were marked with a surge of available resources and a rising tide of both people and dollars that lifted all organizations. The budgets of congregations bulged and the size and number of buildings, along with programs and people to fill them, increased exponentially. The mantra of missional ministry in that past time was "find a need and fill it." If congregations wanted to engage their neighborhood, meet and include new people, and fulfill their missional purpose of changing lives and the world, they were encouraged to find a problem and fix it.

This missional strategy hinged on the congregation's ability to direct resources. If there was a problem of troubled youth in the community, for example, the congregation could start a youth program, host a scouting program, build playgrounds or recreational centers, engage their members in tutoring programs, or any of a host of other initiatives. If there was a problem with hunger in the neighborhood, congregations could quickly initiate pantries, community or school lunch programs, or establish full-blown feeding centers. For the most part, congregations were rich in the resources of dollars and people, which made the role of a provider come naturally as a strategy of their identity and purpose.

But the day of an abundance of resources is now over for most congregations as budgets and attendance continually weakened over the more recent anti-institutional years. Now the conversation about finding a need and filling it feels more like scarcity chasing scarcity. Now a dwindling (and aging) group of leaders in a congregation have committee meetings in which they talk about a need in their neighborhood that calls out to be addressed with more resources. At the same time, they talk about their own unmet budget, their dwindling attendance, and the deferred maintenance on their own buildings. For many congregations, the scarcity seen "out there" is mirrored by the scarcity that leaders struggle with "in here." It is little wonder that so few of these committee meetings end up in operationalized programs, a fresh stream of resources, or any change in the neighborhood. When both the problem and the provider see themselves through the lens of scarcity there is little energy or opportunity to make a difference.

To fit into the new neighborhoods, congregations and their leaders must let go of their old role of being provider and become a participant in the issues and needs of the neighborhood, joining along with what is already being done to make the neighborhood better. The congregation is no longer in the role of bringing God's Spirit to the community, but in getting behind and helping what God's Spirit is already doing.

This requires congregations to break the building and property line assumptions that they are the locus of the holy in a secular world. In the words of a Franciscan monk, "the Medievals built huge ornate churches so that people walking into them would feel like they'd left one world and entered another reality—the Kingdom of God."[12] As humble, plain, or utilitarian as congregational buildings have become over the centuries, the notion that God's Kingdom is located within the property line of the church or the synagogue remained embedded. The established posture of congregations has been to point out into the larger community as the place with problems, reach out with resources to help, and invite those met in the process to step in over the church property line to where the holy could help them as well. God was understood to work from within the congregation as base, using the resources and the people of the congregation who were God's agents in the world. Few in the congregation who saw themselves as providers gave much thought to God being up and about in the neighborhood without them.

As the organizations of the church weakened over time, God's agency in the world did not lessen, and people's search for meaning and purpose for their lives did not wane. People stopped going to "all purpose" places like congregations and instead unbundled their needs and their longings to pursue them in individualistic fashion.[13] Fellowship and support could be found in the cohort of people signed up for Fitbox training or gathered in "third place" coffee shops. Community could be found on Facebook, its later offspring iterations, and ever-expanding Internet sites. Awe and wonder could be sought after in nature, music concerts, and sporting events. Dealing with personal problems happened in small groups of people who all faced the same issues or in not-for-profit help centers that professionally focused on a particular problem or crisis. Wuthnow noted the overall decline of "general purpose organizations" like congregations as individuals moved increasingly to "special-interest groups."[14]

What did not disappear in the past decades, during which congregations struggled with themselves, was the search for purpose and meaning, the importance of community, the need for connection and support and, the impulsive pull of awe and wonder. What did not disappear was God's agency in the world. These simply were no longer limited in people's minds to religion and to the congregation as they had been at an earlier time. Instead of being the provider of all these things, the congregation will now need to seek forms and strategies to reinsert itself as a participant in the larger world outside of itself where all of this seeking continues unabated.

When serving as pastor to the urban Broadway United Methodist Church in Indianapolis, Mike Mather wrestled with this paradigm shift.[15] Instead of looking for people who had problems that he thought he could fix, he helped his congregation search out people who already possessed skills, energy, and hope so that the congregation could invest time, attention, and support in them as they went about the issues of the neighborhood. Instead of hiring staff to take on community problems he employed people to go out in the neighborhood to pull out the talents of those already engaged in the neighborhood. Instead of an outreach committee as part of the organizational structure of the congregation, he introduced a new initiative called the "Animator of the Spirit" that shifted its strategy, in part, from funding emergency assistance in the neighborhood (a resource dependent strategy based on scarcity) to an "Abundance Fund" that strategically paid people to share their gifts with one another in the neighborhood (a sufficiency-based strategy based on the conviction that the gifts and skills needed in the neighborhood are already in place waiting to be discovered). Speaking both for himself and his congregation, Mike wrote that "one of the paradoxes I was learning was that I didn't have to be the lead actor in order to help. Others were much better positioned to do that good work. I could just give it an assist."[16]

If Mike's congregation is one clear example, there are an unknown number of people and congregations learning their own ways past old assumptions that have hampered them in an effort to become participants in what God is already and continually up and doing in communities. Fresh Expressions[17] is a growing collaborative effort to help congregations look outside of themselves in order to take the gifts they already have to the people who are already out there. Others, like Mike Mather, are looking out into the neighborhood to see what God is already doing through people, where resources of skill, hope, courage, and energy are already in place, in order to get involved as supporter and participant. Other individuals, like the Locke Leadership Innovative Leaders,[18] follow the passion for the common good that is already burning within them to build entrepreneurial enterprises of similarly impassioned people in the neighborhood to address at the local level what must be different.

These are only a few examples of the courageous learners, leaders, and early adopters who are moving past the resource restricted (and at times paternalistic) role of being a provider. There is a growing effort afoot in congregations that seek a new role in their neighborhoods as participants in what God is already doing.

The second way for the institutional congregation to reconnect with the neighborhood by resembling its cultural environment is by understanding itself as a *platform* rather than as a *gathering place*.

A central paradox that seemingly inhibits the future of congregations as a neighborhood institution is the long-standing role the congregation has played as a gathering place for the community—the one role that was consistent throughout the American history of congregations. The situation now encountered is that the ripest (perhaps only) level at which the pending cultural value shift toward the common good will be able to find traction is the local level—the neighborhood. The local congregation is a primary neighborhood institution already in place. The congregation is also a natural gathering place, having played that role throughout American history. It would appear that the neighborhood congregation is in its sweet spot, being in the right place at the right time. However, the paradox is that people no longer gather as they once did, and "gathering" itself is no longer defined by location and geography, as described earlier. There is no reason to think that when people in a neighborhood need to connect with one another around shared issues of the common good that they will naturally think of the nearby congregation down the street as the place to do it. In the new digital world, congregations and their buildings have become somewhat invisible on the landscape as a gathering place.

To find its place in this paradox congregations will need, once again, to confront their own dominating assumptions. I have no doubt that congregations will always and forever be a gathering place for worship, prayer, and study. Such reasons to gather are of the very nature of a congregation as an institution of religion. However, worship, prayer, and study are so central to the identity of the congregation that they have led to two dominating assumptions that now limit the role congregations can play in the neighborhood. The one assumption is that the reason people come to a congregation is to fulfill the purpose of the church (i.e., worship, prayer, and study; the activities of faith and faith formation). In other words, it is assumed that the agenda for gathering in a congregation's building belongs to the congregation. The second assumption that has grown in strength from the nostalgic time of growing memberships is that the audience of people who are to gather in the congregation are its "members." That is to say, people have come to believe that to be a welcomed gatherer in a congregation's buildings one must already have (or be willing to establish) an ongoing relationship to the congregation.

To reconnect with its neighborhood by resembling the environment, congregations will need to reexamine two critical issues of agenda and agency. Agenda refers to the reason for which people gather (i.e., to what end?), and agency refers to who has the power to determine what is to be accomplished (i.e., who gets to say what will be done).

To be clear, this shift from gathering place to platform is much less understood than other shifts such as the move from provider to participant. There is less known and fewer examples or experiments to point to. However, this shift is very much driven by the technological, digital environment in which people have learned to seek out places (platforms) that will enable them to address a need that they have defined for themselves and to create a response that they have determined for themselves. The role of platform has become an essential element in how people now gather around their felt needs and their hopes. And the role of platform relinquishes both agenda and agency to the people who use the platform.

A primary technological example of a platform is the Apple iOS digital platform used by all Apple iPhones, iPods, and iPads. The platform very much belongs to the Apple corporation. When customers buy one of the Apple products, they do not purchase the digital platform on which the product works. They cannot open up their iPhone or iPad and tinker with the software to adjust it to their ideas as an owner. Instead of an *owner*, they become a *user* of what belongs to Apple. In a 2014 study of Apple iOS as an example of a platform, it was reported that at that time there were 365 million users (people who purchased an Apple product connecting them to the platform). There were also 800,000 complementary apps developed by non-Apple information and program developers that used the platform but who neither worked for nor were controlled by Apple.[19] The function of the iOS system was simply to provide a place to bring together the 365 million users with the 800,000 apps. The iPhones, iPods, and iPads were platforms where users and apps could be brought together in service to the interests and needs of the users. An offshoot was that not only did the iOS platform become an interface between the user and the provider, it also became a gathering place as users found one another.

Thinking of a congregation as a platform, consider one example of a small, Presbyterian congregation.[20] From an earlier time of a much larger membership and substantial finances, this small congregation had dwindled to a much smaller membership able to afford only a quarter-time interim pastor. It did, however, own a fairly large church building, a manse for the pastor's use, and a plot of ground between the main building and the manse. A lay woman in the congregation asked permission from the governing board to use the plot of ground for a community garden. Permission was given and the woman set out to develop two sets of volunteers from wherever she could find people. The first set of volunteers were to help grow the vegetables in the garden. The second group was trained to give the vegetables away to anyone who came from the neighborhood at appointed times. Signs were put up indicating when vegetables would be given out.

The second group had been trained not only to give the vegetables to the neighbors but to engage them in conversation as well. The volunteers learned the names of neighbors and where they lived. But they also regularly asked these neighbors what most worried them about their neighborhood. One of the strongest patterns of responses focused on the worries and fear people carried about their children. People were very concerned about the lack of opportunities their children had for their future because so few went on to college and so many remained as adults in the area where there were minimal job opportunities.

Rather than try to fix this situation, this small congregation became a platform for people who had a personal investment in the worries.

Neighbors, church members, local school employees, and teachers and students from the education department of the local university were invited into shared conversations. The result was a full-blown tutorial program in collaboration with the local schools and run by volunteers and university students. The local congregation did not determine the issue to work on, did not determine or resource the action that the neighborhood took, and did not "own" the tutorial program that eventually developed. The congregation simply grew vegetables, made friends, hosted conversations, and owned the building where the tutorial program operated.

The congregation served as a platform to bring people together around the people's own shared common good issue. The congregation gave away the agenda and agency to the neighborhood group that formed. It lent resources that it already had to the neighborhood (it's garden plot and building), and, not as a goal but as a byproduct, relationships were formed, attendance at worship began to grow, and the congregation's finances were strengthened. The congregation had become a neighbor by becoming like a familiar part of the environment that people could recognize and knew how to use.

It is worth noting that when a new, part-time clergyperson was called to this congregation, his own personal interest in connecting jazz music to worship settings came along with him. The new pastor turned the congregation's attention away from their vegetable garden and involved them (both attention and resources) in the development of a monthly jazz vesper worship program. Indeed, there were a few new people who found their way to the congregation because they were jazz fans. But the connection to the neighborhood through the tutorial program, as well as the number of neighbors who came to the congregation, dwindled as the new pastor and the congregation took back the agenda, the agency, and the outcomes it would pursue.

The third way for the institutional congregation to reconnect with the neighborhood by resembling its cultural environment is by being a plain speaker rather than a jargon junkie. I write this as a lover of the language of the church. Language is powerful. It directs thought and action. It opens the mind and heart to sensations and aspiration. A full, rich language fills and enriches life. It is no wonder that creative writers labor so intensely over the language that they use. I resonate to the formality and to the image-rich language of the church. Consider the familiar opening prayer of "The Holy Eucharist: Rite One from the Episcopal Church's Book of Common Prayer."

Almighty God, unto whom all hearts are open, all desires known, and from whom no secrets are hid: Cleanse the thoughts of our hearts by the inspiration of thy Holy Spirit, that we may perfectly love thee and worthily magnify thy holy name, through Christ our Lord. Amen.[21]

While being both familiar (English) and unfamiliar (formal and some-what archaic), this language slows me down, it engages both my mind and my feelings, it calls forth images and aspirations. At times when I worship without this language, I miss it. At times when I need to slow down and seek inspiration and aspirations, I go in search of it. It is, bless-edly, part of the jargon of the church.

It is not the language the neighborhood uses. The language of Amer-ican neighborhoods is "plain speak" in its multitude of geographic, ethnic, urban/suburban/rural dialects and variations. During the era of indi-vidualism, the language of the neighborhood has become more coarse, breaking norms of civility and politeness (a-nomos). Through its use on social media, it has been reduced to initialisms so that quick sequences such as lol, bff, or OMG are easily understood as laugh out loud, best friend forever, or oh my God!—all expressions too lengthy for a quick liquid culture to spell out in full.

But the institution of the congregation is slower to change its lan-guage, and it uses its jargon purposefully. In fact, the jargon that the church uses has at least two critical functions that can make it either appropriate or inappropriate depending upon the purpose at hand.

One function of the church's jargon is formation. Jargon is a spe-cialized language used by a profession or a group. It is difficult for others outside the group to understand, but, for those inside the group it carries clear meaning, can invoke aspirations, and direct actions to be taken. Consider the conversation in chapter 6 about discipleship. There was a fairly lengthy discussion in that chapter about God's grace and the Wesleyan system of breaking the understanding of grace into three aspects: prevenient, justifying, and sanctifying. That is pure jargon. Those outside the church and the neighborhood around the church neither need nor respond to the church's way of speaking about such things. But for those who seek formation in the church—those who are seeking conversion to see the world differently and seeking to be in the world differently following hope and sufficiency rather than fear and scarcity—the church's jargon can reshape one's life. It slows down. It gives language to aspirations. It provides thoughtfulness and understanding to experiences. It turns the simplicity of conversion into the rich complexity of discipleship. This is jargon at its best.

But a second function of the church's jargon is to carve out and establish a jurisdiction for a profession and the institutions of that profession as a domain reserved for it alone. It is a way for the church to separate itself from others, claim territory, and establish dominance. In his extensive and rewarding "essay" on professions, Andrew Abbott describes professions as "exclusive occupational groups applying somewhat abstract knowledge to particular cases."[22] The "cases" referred to are reoccurring problems or questions that professions claim for their own professional jurisdiction. In other words, each profession seeks to claim ownership and authority over some set of questions that people will then need to come to them for answers. The profession of law formed initially around questions of property rights so that anyone with questions about ownership or the transfer of ownership of property would need the help of a lawyer. The profession of medicine shaped its jurisdiction of control over questions of sickness and disease. The professions of finance claimed their jurisdiction over participation in the institutions of the economy. The jurisdiction of the professional clergy and the institutions of religion focus on questions of meaning, purpose, community, and mystery. Jurisdiction is the territory of a profession's authority in which the questions that the profession addresses form the boundary that protects the profession from the incursion of other professions and from the meddling of amateurs.[23] Jargon is a major tool of professional jurisdiction. It makes the practitioners of the profession indispensable. People are wise to consult a lawyer before signing an important contract because it is difficult to translate rights and restrictions hidden in the legal jargon of the contract.

Abbott's work is a fascinating study of the malleability of, and the contest over, the boundaries of a profession and the importance of jargon in protecting boundaries. The jargon of the church both gives congregations a way to speak of important things (formation) and also protects the church's claim against other competitors such as individualism, consumerism, the social justice movement, techno-utopianism, and atavism (separation). The dilemma is that while the esoteric nature of jargon offers a way to speak of important things and protects against false claims from other sources, it also excludes the uninitiated. Used too freely it becomes a barrier to being understood in the neighborhood. To introduce oneself in the neighborhood with a theological vocabulary or with Jesus language makes the congregation a suspicious intruder, not a neighbor.

In all cases, the jargon of a profession and of the institutions of that profession is a tool of power and authority used to establish and maintain boundaries. Managing that power and protecting the boundaries of the profession makes people involved into jargon junkies. The more that jargon is used, the greater the distance from the culture and the stronger the barrier separating the institutions of the profession from the culture. The first rule of the missionary is to learn the indigenous language of the people one will be with; to be a participant in the neighborhood the congregation will first need to speak plainly, bluntly, and quickly—just as the neighbors do. A culture in crisis needs to hear of hope, sufficiency, and community in understandable ways.

It is clear that to be accepted in the neighborhood as a trusted participant, the congregation will need to give up the power and the authority that protects its claim to know what others do not. It is sufficient for the congregation to simply and plainly *say what it sees differently* from others. It is more powerful for the people of the congregation to simply and plainly *be different* from others because of the hope, sufficiency, and community that they have found. When living in the indigenous neighborhood it is critical to participate in ways that are understood and do not exclude others as equals. The jargon of the church—the beautiful, expressive, aspirational, blessed way of speaking of hope—will always be there for those who choose formation. As a participant in the neighborhood, power and authority that comes with specialized languages must first be given away in order to meet others as equals. Truth and hope will show through as the disciples from the congregation lean into the common good by living in ways that challenge the competing claims of fear and scarcity.

Letting Go

In this next cultural turning when institutions will continue to be mistrusted but nonetheless will still be critically needed, the first difficult step that leaders will need to take is that of letting go. As congregations seek to find both their place and their voice in the neighborhood, the new varieties and expressions of congregations will find shape only by letting go of old assumptions and the practices that have become constraints. It is not by accident that the new learnings of congregations described here are reported as "rather thans": participant *rather than* provider; platform *rather than* gathering place; plain speak *rather than* jargon. Any step into the new requires first letting go of the old.

In his wonderfully helpful work on transitions, William Bridges identified three stages at the foundation of all transitional change: (1) Endings (the critical work of letting go of what has ended); (2) the Neutral Zone (the confusion of the in-between time); and (3) Making a Beginning.[24] The wise insight from his work is that people always want to start with stage 3 by jumping into new beginnings with conviction and clarity, as if they know what they are doing. Stage 1 of letting go is hard and difficult work and people actively try to avoid it. It is laborious to have to unearth assumptions that we aren't even aware of but give us a false sense of knowing what we are doing. To unearth and disclaim these assumptions and practices leaves us feeling vulnerable, not easily sure of what to think and do without them. If and when the work of stage 1 is done we enter into stage 2, the time of confusion that comes with being in the in-between time. We have let go of that which we do know but which does not help anymore. Without what we were once sure of, we now are faced with being uncertain of what to do. Bridges pointed out that people naturally avoid the hard work of stage 1—but then they also deny the need to enter into the confusion of stage 2, the Neutral Zone. It is more comforting to be certain, even when wrong. But letting go and the confusion that follows is necessary to new starts. In order for the new forms of institutional congregations to be the trusted institutions needed for the next cultural turning, in order for it to lean into the reestablishment of a common good, leaders will need to make themselves comfortable with *ignoramus*, with the confusion of not knowing what to do next. That was how the Israelites made it through the wilderness. It is the way to start new.

Tikkun Olam—The Repair of the World

There is within Judaism the concept of Tikkun olam, which refers to efforts and actions meant to repair or improve the world. There have always been jests that since God created the world in six days, it was somewhat of a rush job and the whole cloth of creation had some slipped stitches, a few tears, and a hole or two left unnoticed. The reality is that creation is a complete gift. It is a self-balancing, life-sustaining system of interwoven and interdependent animate and inanimate necessities that create together the very world that sustains all that we know. It came before us and will be after us. So, that while we are here it falls to us to find and follow those patterns of repair and rebalancing that must go on continually. Tikkun olam is that effort given to repairing the social order that allows people to be a healthy part of the gift of creation.

The work of repair and maintenance cannot be done without institutions. As far as the church is concerned, the origin of its institutional form began with Jesus himself who taught truth and values and infused his teaching and selection of the disciples with symbolic meaning.[25] With Jesus, the disciples then organized themselves institutionally. Along with the earliest congregations, these first Christians understood the importance of differentiated leadership roles, agreements and norms, and standard practices. It is the way in which truth, once found, can be carried forward. Usufruct.

To have lived through a time of anti-institutionalism (as natural as it is in an oscillating culture), to have overemphasized and overvalued the liberties and the claims of individualism, to have accepted a-nomos with its dismissal of the very norms that give us a way to live together with one another, we are now in a time that needs repair. The repair and rebalancing that is needed will be provided by the institutions of morality so that it is now more than ever that we need the sturdy *institutional* congregation even while we are searching for the new forms of the *organizational* congregation. Housed in the institutional congregation are the values that need attending, the simple truths that have gone missing. Consider Rabbi Sacks' succinct conclusion:

> *Love your neighbor. Love the stranger. Hear the cry of the otherwise unheard. Liberate the poor from their poverty. Care for the dignity of all. Let those who have more than they need share their blessings with those who have less. Feed the hungry, house the homeless, and heal the sick in body and mind. Fight injustice, whoever it is done by and whoever it is done against. And do these things because, being human, we are bound by a covenant of human solidarity, whatever our color or culture, class or Creed.*
>
> *These are moral principles, not economic or political ones. They have to do with conscience, not wealth or power. But without them, freedom will not survive.*[26]

That is pure usufruct. Let the church speak.

NOTES

AN INTRODUCTION TO AN ARGUMENT

1. Tara Isabella Burton, *Strange Rites: New Religions for a Godless World* (New York: Public Affairs, 2020).

2. Ibid., 190.

3. Loren Mead, *The Once and Future Church: Reinventing the Congregation for a New Mission Frontier* (Bethesda: The Alban Institute, 1991).

4. Will Herberg, *Protestant–Catholic–Jew: An Essay on American Religious Sociology* (Chicago: The University of Chicago Press, 1960).

5. Émile Durkheim, *The Elementary Forms of Religious Life* (New York: Free Press, 1995).

6. Rex Miller, *The Millennial Matrix: Reclaiming the Past, Reframing the Future of the Church* (San Francisco: Jossey-Bass, 2004)

7. Robert Bellah, William Sullivan, Ann Swidler, and Steven Topton, *Habits of the Heart: Individualism and Commitment in American Life* (New York: Harper & Row, Publishers, 1985), 221, 235.

8. David Moore, *The Other British Isles* (London: McFarland & Co., Inc., 2005), 35.

9. Moisés Naím, *The End of Power: From Boardrooms to Battlefields and Churches to States, Why Being in Charge Isn't What It Used to Be* (New York: Basic Books, 2013).

CHAPTER 1

1. Thomas Friedman, *That Used to Be Us: How America Fell Behind in the World It Invented and How We Can Come Back* (New York: Farrar, Straus and Giroux, 2011).

2. Gil Rendle, *Quietly Courageous: Leading the Church in a Changing World* (Lanham: Rowman & Littlefield, 2019), 19–53.

3. Gil Rendle, *Journey in the Wilderness: New Life for Mainline Churches* (Nashville: Abingdon Press, 2010), 17–57.

4. Gil Rendle and Alice Mann, *Holy Conversations: Strategic Planning as a Spiritual Practice for Congregations* (Bethesda: The Alban Institute, 2003), 3–5.

5. H. Richard Niebuhr, *Christ and Culture* (San Francisco: HarperSanFrancisco, 2001).

6. Timothy Snyder, *On Tyranny: Twenty Lessons from the Twentieth Century* (New York: Tim Duggan Books, 2017), 22.

Chapter 2

1. Dorothy Bass, "Congregations and the Bearing of Traditions," in *American Congregations, Volume Two: New Perspectives in the Study of Congregations*, edited by James Wind and James Lewis (Chicago: The University of Chicago Press, 1994), 169–91.

2. Gibson Winter, *The Suburban Captivity of the Churches; An Analysis of Protestant Responsibility in the Expanding Metropolis* (Chicago: The University of Chicago Press, 1967).

3. E. Brooks Holifield, "Toward a History of American Congregations," in *American Congregations, Volume Two: New Perspectives in the Study of Congregations*, edited by James Wind and James Lewis (Chicago: The University of Chicago Press, 1994), 23–53.

4. Ibid., 33.

5. Ibid., 39.

6. Langdon Gilkey, "The Christian Congregation as a Religious Community," in *American Congregations, Volume Two: New Perspectives in the Study of Congregations*, edited by James Wind and James Lewis (Chicago: The University of Chicago Press, 1994), 106.

7. Walter Brueggemann, *The Creative Word: Canon as a Model for Biblical Education* (Minneapolis: Fortress Press, 2015), 28.

Chapter 3

1. Phyllis Tickle, *The Great Emergence: How Christianity Is Changing and Why* (Grand Rapids, MI: Baker Books, 2008).

2. Zygmunt Bauman, *Liquid Times: Living in an Age of Uncertainty* (Cambridge, UK: Polity Press, 2007).

3. William Strauss and Neil Howe, *The Fourth Turning: What the Cycles of History Tell Us About America's Next Rendezvous with Destiny* (New York: Broadway Books, 1997).

4. Daniel Yankelovich, *New Rules: Searching for Self-Fulfillment in a World Turned Upside Down* (New York: Bantam Books, 1982).

5. Hugh Heclo, *On Thinking Institutionally* (Boulder, CO: Paradigm Publications, 2008).

6. Jonathan Sacks, *Morality: Restoring the Common Good in Divided Times.* (New York: Basic Books, 2020).

7. Robert Putnam, *The Upswing: How America Came Together a Century Ago and How We Can Do It Again* (New York: Simon and Schuster, 2020).

8. Jenny Odell, *How to Do Nothing: Resisting the Attention Economy* (Brooklyn, NY: Melville House, 2019).

9. Bruce Reed, *The Task of the Church and the Role of Its Members* (Bethesda, MD: The Alban Institute, 1984).

10. Robert Putnam, *The Upswing: How America Came Together a Century Ago and How We Can Do It Again* (New York: Simon & Schuster, 2020), 2.

11. Ibid., 12.

12. Ken Wilber, *Trump and a Post-Truth World* (Boulder, CO: Shambhala Publications, Inc., 2017), 3–4.

13. See: Ken Wilber, *A Theory of Everything: An Integral Vision for Business, Politics, Science, and Spirituality* (Boulder, CO: Shambhala Publications, Inc., 2017).

14. Leonard Kageler, email of 10/5/18.

15. *The United Methodist Hymnal* (Nashville: the United Methodist Publishing House, 1989), 577.

16. Wilber, *Trump and a Post-Truth World*, 4–5.

17. Odell, *How to Do Nothing*.

18. Walter Brueggemann, *The Creative Word: Canon as a Model for Biblical Education* (Minneapolis, MN: Fortress Press, 2015), 53.

19. Ibid., 28.

20. Margaret Wheatley, *Who Do We Choose to Be? Facing Reality, Claiming Leadership, Restoring Sanity* (Oakland, CA: Berrett-Koehler Publications, 2017).

CHAPTER 4

1. Hugh Heclo, *On Thinking Institutionally* (Boulder: Paradigm Publishers, 2008), 110.

2. Ibid., 47.

3. Rabbi Nossen Scherman and Rabbi Meir Zlotowitz, General Editors, *The Chamash: The Torah—Haftaros and Five Megillos with a Commentary Antologized From the Rabbinic Writings* (Brookline: Mesorah Publications, LTD, 1998), 406.

4. Ibid., 411.

5. Ibid., 416.

6. Ibid., 25.

7. Jonathan Sacks, *Morality: Restoring the Common Good in Divided Times* (New York: Basic Books, 2020), 11, 18.

8. Margaret Wheatley, *Who Do We Choose to Be?* (San Francisco: Bennet-Koehler Publishers, 2017), 20, 36, 72–74.

9. Sacks, *Morality*, 16.

10. Ibid., 25

11. Heclo, *On Thinking Institutionally*, 38.

12. Sacks, *Morality*, 32.

13. John Silber, *Seeking the North Star: Selected Speeches* (Boston, David R. Godine, Publisher, 2014), 140–49.

14. Stephen L. Carter, *Civility: Manners, Morals, and the Etiquette of Democracy* (New York: Basic Books, 1998).

15. Heclo, *On Thinking Institutionally*, 62–63.

16. Ibid., 25.

17. Ibid, 38.

18. Tara Isabella Burton, *Strange Rites: New Religions for a Godless World* (New York: Public Affairs, 2020), 161–64.

19. David Brooks, "How To Destroy Truth," *New York Times*, July 1, 2021.

20. Brian Doyle, *One Long River of Song* (New York: Back Bay Books, 2019), 224.

21. Heclo, *On Thinking Institutionally*.

22. Heclo, ibid., 19–22.

23. Robert Quinn, *Deep Change: Discovering the Leader Within* (San Francisco: Jossey-Bass, 1996).

24. Gil Rendle, *Quietly Courageous: Leading the Church in a Changing World* (Lanham, MD: Rowman & Littlefield Publishers, 2019).

25. Heclo, *On Thinking Institutionally*, 162.

26. Sacks, *Morality*, 34.

27. Heclo, *On Thinking Institutionally*, 160.

CHAPTER 5

1. Roger Olsen, pathos.com/blogs/rogereolson/2013/01/did-karl-barth-really-say-jesus-loves-me-this-i-know.

2. Ken Wilber, *Trump and a Post-Trump World* (Boulder: Shambhala Press, 2017), 3.

3. William Sloane Coffin, *Credo* (Louisville: Westminster John Knox Press, 2004), 93.

4. Jonathan Sacks, *Morality: Restoring the Common Good in Divided Times* (New York: Basic Books, 2020), 34.

5. Thomas Long, *Testimony: Talking Ourselves Into Being Christian* (San Francisco: Jossey-Bass, 2004), 44.

6. Joseph Turrow, *Breaking Up America: Advertisers and the New Media World* (Chicago: The University of Chicago Press, 1997).

7. Lynne Twist, *The Soul of Money: Reclaiming the Wealth of Our Inner Resources* (New York: W. W. Norton & Co., 2003), 43–44.

8. Yuval Levin, *The Fractured Republic: Renewing America's Social Contract in the Age of Individualism* (New York: Basic Books, 2016).

9. Tara Isabelle Burton, *Strange Rites: New Religions for a Godless World* (New York: Public Affairs, 2020), 94–95.

10. Walter Brueggemann, *The Word That Redescribes the World: The Bible and Discipleship* (Minneapolis: Fortress Press, 2011), xiii.

11. Joel Green, General Editor, *The Common English Study Bible* (Nashville: The United Methodist Publishing House, 2013), 49NT.

12. Richard Hays, *Echoes of Scripture in the Gospels* (Waco: Baylor University Press, 2016), 123.

13. N. T. Wright, *Paul: A Biography* (New York: Harper One, 2018), 44–53.

14. Ibid., 79.

15. Ibid., 368.

CHAPTER 6

1. Rueben Job, *Three Simple Rules: A Wesleyan Way of Living* (Nashville: Abingdon Press, 2007).

2. Ibid., 21.

3. https://homeboyindustries.org

4. Rabbi Nossen Scherman and Rabbi Meir Zlotowitz, General Editors, *The Torah: Haftoros and Five Megillos with a Commentary Anthologized From the Rabbinic Writings* (New York: Mesorah Publications, 2000), 412.

5. Scott Jones, *The Extreme Center* (Nashville: Abingdon Press, 2002), 157.

6. Ibid., 182.

7. Ibid., 196.

8. *Book of Discipline of the United Methodist Church* (Nashville: The United Methodist Publishing House, 2016), P.104; 81.

9. Leonora Tubbs Tisdale, *Preaching as Local Theology and Folk Art* (Minneapolis: Fortress Press), xii.

10. Brian Doyle, *One Long River of Song* (New York: Back Bay Books, 2019), xix.

11. Barry Johnson, *Polarity Management: Identifying and Managing Unsolvable Problems* (Amherst: HRD Press, 1992), xii.

12. Ibid., 23.

13. Timothy Snyder, *On Tyranny: Twenty Lessons from the Twentieth Century* (New York: Tim Duggan Books, 2017), 81.

14. Joseph Turow, *Breaking Up America* (Chicago: The University of Chicago Press, 1997).

CHAPTER 7

1. Margaret Wheatley, *Who Do We Choose to Be? Facing Reality, Claiming Leadership, Restoring Sanity* (San Francisco: Berrett-Koehler Publishers, Inc., 2017), Introduction.

2. Moisés Naím, *The End of Power: From Boardrooms to Battlefields and Churches to States, Why Being in Charge Isn't What It Used to Be* (New York: Basic Books, 2013).

3. Marc Dunkelman, *The Vanishing Neighbor: The Transformation of American Community* (New York: W.W. Norton & Company, 2014), 46.

4. Ibid., 90–94.

5. Ibid., 97.

6. Ibid., 97.

7. Ibid., 104.

8. Ibid., 107.

9. Jay Pathak and Dave Runyon, *The Art of Neighboring: Building Genuine Relationships Right Outside Your Door* (Grand Rapids: Baker Books, 2012), 36.

10. Blair Thompson-White, "Could Imitation Be a Step on Our Path Toward Creating the New Church" (https://tmf-fdn.org/lm-blogs/imitation).

CHAPTER 8

1. Yuval Noah Harari, *Sapiens: A Brief History of Humankind* (New York: Harper Collins Publishers, 2015), 250.

2. Ibid., 286.

3. William Strauss and Neil Howe, *The Fourth Turning: What the Cycles of History Tell Us About America's Next Rendezvous with Destiny* (New York: Broadway Books, 1997), 3.

4. Ibid., 112.

5. Ibid., 255.

6. Gil Rendle, *Quietly Courageous: Leading the Church in a Changing World* (Lanham: Rowman & Littlefield, 2019), 156–67.

7. Michael Crichton, *The Lost World* (New York: Ballantine Publishing Group, 1995).

8. Bishop Janice Riggle Huie, "Reservoirs of Resilience in Uncertain Times: Reflections on Hope, Courage, and Purpose" (https://tmf-fdn.org/white-papers/reservoirs-of -resilience), 24.

9. Ibid., 6.

10. Ibid., 6.

11. Robert Wuthnow, *Loose Connections: Joining Together in America's Fragmented Communities* (Cambridge: Harvard University Press, 1998), 7.

12. Ian Morgan Cron, *Chasing Francis: A Pilgrim's Tale* (Grand Rapids: Zondervan, 2006), 96.

13. Angie Thurston and Casper ter Kuile, "Faithful," How We Gather, 2017, https:// sacred.design/wp-content/uploads/2019/10/How_We_Gather_Digital_4.11.17.pdf.

14. Wuthnow, *Loose Connections*, 15.

15. Michael Mather, *Finding Abundant Communities in Unexpected Places* (Grand Rapids: William B. Eerdmans Publishing Co., 2018).

16. Ibid., 22.

17. http://freshexpressions.com

18. http://wesleyanimpactpartners.org

19. Amrit Tiwana, *Platform Ecosystems: Aligning Architecture, Governance, and Strategy* (Boston: Morgan Kaufman, 2014), 5.

20. As reported by Rev. Allen Timm, retired executive Presbyter of the Detroit Presbytery of the Presbyterian Church.

21. *The Book of Common Prayer* (New York: Church Publishing Inc., 2007), 323.

22. Andrew Abbott, *The Systems of Professions: An Essay on the Division of Expert Labor* (Chicago: The University of Chicago Press, 1988), 8.

23. Ibid., 2, 37, 280–300.

24. William Bridges, *Transitions: Making Sense of Life's Changes* (Reading: Addison-Wesley Publishing Co., 1980).

25. Kavin Rowe, *Christianity's Surprise: A Sure and Certain Hope* (Nashville: Abingdon Press, 2020) 55.

26. Jonathan Sacks, *Morality: Restoring the Common Good in Divided Times* (New York: Basic Books), x.

Bibliography

Abbott, Andrew. *The Systems of Professions: An Essay on the Division of Expert Labor.* Chicago: The University of Chicago Press, 1988.

Bass, Dorothy. "Congregations and the Bearing of Traditions." In *American Congregations, Volume Two: New Perspectives in the Study of Congregations*, edited by James Wind and James Lewis, 169–91. Chicago: University of Chicago Press, 1994.

Bauman, Zygmunt. *Liquid Times: Living in an Age of Uncertainty.* Cambridge: Polity Press, 2007.

Bellah, Robert, William Sullivan, Ann Swidler, and Steven Topton. *Habits of the Heart: Individualism and Commitment in American Life.* New York: Harper & Row, Publishers, 1985.

Book of Common Prayer. New York: Church Publishing Inc., 2007.

Book of Discipline of the United Methodist Church. Nashville, TN: The United Methodist Publishing House, 2016.

Bridges, William. *Transitions: Making Sense of Life's Changes.* Reading: Addison—Wesley Publishing Co, 1980.

Brooks, David. "How To Destroy Truth." *New York Times*, July 1, 2021.

Brueggemann, Walter. *The Creative Word: Canon as a Model for Biblical Education.* Minneapolis: Fortress Press, 2015.

Brueggemann, Walter. *The Word That Redescribes the World: The Bible and Discipleship.* Minneapolis: Fortress Press, 2011.

Burton, Tara Isabella. *Strange Rites: New Religions for a Godless World.* New York: Public Affairs, 2020.

Carter, Stephen L. *Civility: Manners, Morals, and the Etiquette of Democracy.* New York: Basic Books, 1998.

Crichton, Michael. *The Lost World.* New York: Ballantine Publishing Group, 1995.

Coffin, William Sloane. *Credo.* Louisville: Westminster John Knox Press, 2004.

Cron, Ian Morgan. *Chasing Francis: A Pilgrim's Tale.* Grand Rapids: Zondervan, 2006.

Doyle, Brian. *One Long River of Song.* New York: Back Bay Books, 2019.

Dunkelman, Marc. *The Vanishing Neighbor: The Transformation of American Community.* New York: W.W. Norton & Company, 2014.

Durkheim, Émile. *The Elementary Forms of Religious Life.* New York: Free Press, 1995.

Friedman, Thomas. *That Used to Be Us: How America Fell Behind in the World It Invented and How We Can Come Back.* New York: Farrar, Straus, and Giroux, 2011.

Gilkey, Langdon. "The Christian Congregation as a Religious Community." In *American Congregations, Volume Two: New Perspectives in the Study of Congregations*, edited by James Wind and James Lewis, 100–32. Chicago: The University of Chicago Press, 1994.

Green, Joel (ed.). *The Common English Study Bible*. Nashville: The United Methodist Publishing House, 2013.

Harari, Yuval Noah. *Sapiens: A Brief History of Humankind*. New York: Harper Collins Publishers, 2015.

Hays, Richard. *Echoes of Scripture in the Gospels*. Waco: Baylor University Press, 2016.

Heclo, Hugh. *On Thinking Institutionally*. Boulder, CO: Paradigm Publications, 2008.

Herberg, Will. *Protestant–Catholic–Jew: An Essay on American Religious Sociology*. Chicago: The University of Chicago Press, 1960.

Holifield, E. Brooks. "Toward a History of American Congregations." In *American Congregations, Volume Two: New Perspectives in the Study of Congregations*, edited by James Wind and James Lewis, 23–53. Chicago: The University of Chicago Press, 1994.

Huie, Janice Riggle. "Reservoirs of Resilience in Uncertain Times: Reflections on Hope, Courage, and Purpose." https://tmf-fdn.org/white-papers/reservoirs-of-resilience.

Job, Ruben. *Three Simple Rules: A Wesleyan Way of Living*. Nashville: Abingdon Press, 2007.

Johnson, Barry. *Polarity Management: Identifying and Managing Unsolvable Problems*. Amherst: HRD Press, 1992.

Jones, Scott. *The Extreme Center*. Nashville: Abingdon Press, 2002.

Levin, Yuval. *The Fractured Republic: Renewing America's Social Contract in the Age of Individualism*. New York: Basic Books, 2016.

Long, Thomas. *Testimony: Talking Ourselves Into Being Christian*. San Francisco: Jossey-Bass, 2004.

Mather, Michael. *Finding Abundant Communities in Unexpected Places*. Grand Rapids: William B. Eerdmans Publishing Co., 2018.

Mead, Loren. *The Once and Future Church: Reinventing the Congregation for a New Mission Frontier*. Bethesda: The Alban Institute, 1991.

Miller, Rex. *The Millennial Matrix: Reclaiming the Past, Reframing the Future of the Church*. San Francisco: Jossey-Bass, 2004.

Niebuhr, H. Richard. *Christ and Culture*. San Francisco: HarperSanFrancisco, 2001.

Moore, David. *The Other British Isles*. London: McFarland & Co., Inc., 2005.

Naím, Moisés. *The End of Power: From Boardrooms to Battlefields and Churches to States, Why Being in Charge Isn't What It Used to Be*. New York: Basic Books, 2013.

Odell, Jenny. *How To Do Nothing: Resisting the Attention Economy*. Brooklyn: Melville House, 2019.

Olsen, Roger. "Did Karl Barth Really Say Jesus Loves Me, This I Know . . ." https://www.patheos.com/blogs/rogereolson/2013/01/did-karl-barth-really-say-jesus-loves-me-this-i-know/.

Pathak, Jay and Dave Runyon. *The Art of Neighboring: Building Genuine Relationships Right Outside Your Door*. Grand Rapids: Baker Books, 2012.

Putnam, Robert. *The Upswing: How America Came Together a Century Ago and How We Can Do It Again.* New York: Simon and Schuster, 2020.

Quinn, Robert. *Deep Change: Discovering the Leader Within.* San Francisco: Jossey-Bass, 1996.

Reed, Bruce. *The Task of the Church and the Role of Its Members,* Bethesda: The Alban Institute, 1984.

Rendle, Gil. *Journey in the Wilderness: New Life for Mainline Churches.* Nashville: Abingdon Press, 2010.

Rendle, Gil. *Quietly Courageous: Leading the Church in a Changing World.* Lanham: Rowman & Littlefield, 2019.

Rendle, Gil, and Alice Mann. *Holy Conversations: Strategic Planning as a Spiritual Practice for Congregations.* Bethesda, MD: The Alban Institute, 2003.

Rowe, Kavin. *Christianity's Surprise: A Sure and Certain Hope.* Nashville: Abingdon Press, 2020.

Sacks, Jonathan. *Morality: Restoring the Common Good in Divided Times.* New York: Basic Books, 2020.

Scherman, Rabbi Nossen and Rabbi Meir Zlotowitz, General Editors. *The Chamash: The Torah—Haftaros and Five Megillos with a Commentary Antologized from the Rabbinic Writings.* Brookline, NY: Mesorah Publications, Ltd., 1998.

Silber, John. *Seeking the North Star: Selected Speeches.* Boston: David R. Godine, Publisher, 2014.

Snyder, Timothy. *On Tyranny: Twenty Lessons from the Twentieth Century.* New York: Tim Duggan Books, 2017.

Strauss, William and Neil Howe, *The Fourth Turning: What the Cycles of History Tell Us About America's Next Rendezvous with Destiny.* New York: Broadway Books, 1997.

Thompson-White, Blair. "Could Imitation Be a Step on Our Path Toward Creating the New Church," https://tmf-fdn.org/lm-blogs/imitation.

Thurston, Angie and Casper ter Kuile, "Faithful," *How We Gather,* 2017, https://sacred.design/wp-content/uploads/2019/10/How_We_Gather_Digital_4.11.17.pdf.

Tickle, Phyllis. *The Great Emergence: How Christianity Is Changing and Why.* Grand Rapids, MI: Baker Books, 2008.

Tisdale, Leonora Tubbs. *Preaching as Local Theology and Folk Art.* Minneapolis: Fortress-Press, 1997.

Tiwana, Amrit. *Platform Ecosystems: Aligning Architecture, Governance, and Strategy.* Boston: Morgan Kaufman, 2014.

Turrow, Joseph. *Breaking Up America: Advertisers and the New Media World.* Chicago: The University of Chicago Press, 1997.

Twist, Lynne. *The Soul of Money: Reclaiming the Wealth of Our Inner Resources.* New York: W. W. Norton & Co., 2003.

United Methodist Hymnal. Nashville: The United Methodist Publishing House, 1989.

Wheatley, Margaret. *Who Do We Choose to Be? Facing Reality, Claiming Leadership, Restoring Sanity.* Oakland: Berrett-Koehler Publications, 2017.

Wilber, Ken. *A Theory of Everything: An Integral Vision for Business, Politics, Science, and Spirituality.* Boulder: Shambhala Publications, Inc., 2017.

Wilber, Ken. *Trump and a Post-Truth World*. Boulder, CO: Shambhala Publications, Inc., 2017.

Winter, Gibson. *The Suburban Captivity of the Churches; An Analysis of Protestant Responsibility in the Expanding Metropolis*. Chicago: The University of Chicago Press, 1967.

Wright, N. T. *Paul: A Biography*. New York: Harper One, 2018.

Wuthnow, Robert. *Loose Connections: Joining Together in America's Fragmented Communities*. Cambridge, MA: Harvard University Press, 1998.

Yankelovich, Daniel. *New Rules: Searching for Self-Fulfillment in a World Turned Upside Down*. New York: Bantam Books, 1982.

INDEX

613 Mosaic commandments,
79–80;
dual commandment, 81;
Ten Commandments, 106.
See usufruct
common good, xiii, xviii, 5, 19,
29–30, 35, 41–42, 51, 70–71,
100, 135
congregation:
as "bearer of tradition," 12;
Comprehensive
Congregation, 15–16;
as countercultural
institution, 4–5;
Devotional Congregation,
16–17, 107;
hubris of congregations,
xvii, 2;
as invisible neighbor, 125;
as mediating institution, 12;
membership decline, 33;
as platform organization,
146–148;
Social Congregation, 17–18;
Participatory Congregation,
18–19
constructive freshness vs. critical
certainty, 98
conversion, 83, 102–104
Crichton, Michael, 138
cultural value systems, 27, 30
culture war, 36, 46–47

D
de Tocqueville, Alex, 32, 35

discipleship, 87, 92–93, 104;
from principle to practice,
93–94;
from simple to complex,
94–96;
foundation and context,
96–97
Doyle, Brian, 58, 99
Duncan, James David, 99
Dunkelman, Marc, 117–120, 121
Durkheim, Emile, xiii

F
fascism, 8
"find a need and fill it," 141
formation, 48, 149–150
Fosdick, Harry Emerson, 37
Fresh Expressions, 126, 144
Friedman, Thomas, 1

G
general theory of religion (Grubb
Institute), 30. *See* oscillation
generosity, 93
Gilded Age (1870–1890), 35, 37
Gilkey, Langdon, 22
Global Methodist Church, 98
Glubb, Sir John, 52
grace, 94;
as jargon, 150;
justifying, 94–95;
prevenient, 94–95;
sanctifying, 95–96
gun culture and control, xvi, 23

ABOUT THE AUTHOR

Gil Rendle is former senior vice president for the Texas Methodist Foundation as well as former senior consultant and director of consulting for the Alban Institute. As an ordained minister with a PhD in organizational and group dynamics, he has worked with Protestant, Catholic, and Jewish congregations and denominational systems for more than forty years. He is the author of a number of books, including *Quietly Courageous: Leading the Church in a Changing World*. He lives in Haverford, Pennsylvania, with his wife, Lynne.

Made in the USA
Middletown, DE
16 August 2023